Everything <u>You</u> Need to Know About

House Training

Puppies & Adult Dogs

Everything <u>You</u> Need to Know About

House Training

Puppies & Adult Dogs

Lori Verni,
Certified Master Dog Trainer

A Best Paw Forward Book

Everything You Need to Know About House Training
Puppies & Adult Dogs

A Best Paw Forward Book

April 2005

ISBN 1 - 4116 - 3153 - 6

Contents

Acknowledgments

As I arrive at the goal of publishing this book, I realize that there are several people to whom I owe my sincere thanks and appreciation for their support, expertise, and encouragment throughout this journey.

To all of the veterinarians, groomers, rescue personnel, and clients who have put their trust in me throughout the years, I thank you for giving me the opportunity to work with so many beloved family pets.

Special thanks is also expressed to Brian Krapf of Low Fat Designs whose expertise and encouragement helped me to put this project together.

To my editor, proofreader, and lifelong friend Clarice Joos, I thank you for your painstaking efforts in giving my book its finishing touches. Your friendship and support have meant the world to me for many years.

My friend Leslie Lido receives my appreciation for (unknowingly) inspiring me to become a professional writer in the first place.

To all of the editors who have published my work over the years, I thank you for the experience and the income.

To my parents, I thank you for believing in me, and for being such wonderful grandparents to my children.

And last but not least, I thank my husband Frank. Without your support, I could never have pulled this off. Your unwavering understanding of all the hours I've spent at the computer while you've picked up some of the slack with our business, the kids, and the house is appreciated more than you'll ever know.

Thank You!

Introduction

Without a doubt, housebreaking is an issue that is of top priority to every dog owner. Pets can be a very enjoyable part of life...but not as much if your carpets, furniture or other items are being ruined!

We all expect a puppy to require house training. But there are many adult dogs with housebreaking issues too! Over the years, I've worked with dogs as old as 11 years that have never been completely house trained before! I've also worked with hundreds of puppies and adult dogs whose owners have been trying for months and months to train them.

It doesn't need to be so difficult! In fact, having personally housebroken (in my own home) dozens of dogs, I know that by following the methods you're about to learn, any dog can be house trained in just a few weeks. Yes, even a Bichon Frise or a Beagle (often rumored to be "untrainable"), and even an older dog who has had confusion in this area for years.

In this book, we'll address every aspect of housebreaking for both puppies and older dogs. Many common issues will be covered in great detail, as well as plenty of problems that are not so common.

My goal is for you to understand how dogs think with regard to house training. You'll then be able to use that knowledge to prevent or alleviate housebreaking problems with your pet, increasing enjoyment and eliminating resentment.

As a Certified Master Dog Trainer with over 10 years of experience, I've worked with over 2,600 dogs and their families. They're all "regular family pets" just like yours and mine. Some simply needed some obedience, housebreaking, or manners, and others have had very serious behavior problems such as separation anxiety, aggression, or wild behavior.

Since I am a "regular person" as well as a dog trainer, the methods I teach are easily adaptable to fit each household's specific needs and schedule. As a Mom, I understand the concerns that are particular to homes with children. While it may be great in theory to recommend three hours a day of practicing with your dog, for most people this would be impractical.

Therefore, you will find the methods contained in this book to be highly adaptable to your own lifestyle.

However, if you're looking for a magical solution, I must admit, I've misplaced my magic wand! The fact is, house training your pet is going to involve some work on your part.

I could claim that your dog will be house trained in a weekend or a week. However, that would be unrealistic and highly unlikely to provide honorable results.

In my opinion, "house trained" does not mean "starting to catch on." It means "finished." Trustworthy. No accidents. And using a designated area outdoors.

By following the methods contained in this book, your dog can realistically, within 30 days, understand all of the following: all bathroom business is to be done outdoors, in a designated area. Eliminating, leg lifting, or other soiling is not allowed indoors in any part of the house. Trustworthy. Done.

Let's begin!

Part I

How to Teach

Your Dog

A Quick Note About Male and Female

As you continue throughout this book, you'll notice that I consistently refer to dogs in the male context, as in "him", "he" or "his." Of course, I realize that many people reading this book may have a female dog. All of the concepts and methods apply to both males and females.

However, in the interest of keeping things simple, instead of constantly saying "him or her," "he or she," etc., I've decided to use the old-fashioned method of using a generic male format. There is no insult intended to all the female dog owners of the world. I hope you are not offended. Thank you.

Understanding How Dogs Think

When it comes to house training, one of the most important things to understand is how your pet thinks. Dogs are innately clean animals, who by nature prefer to have separate areas for eating, sleeping, and eliminating. If you were to study dogs in the wild (wolves, wild dogs, etc.) they instinctively have one area where they eat, sleep, or play (their den), and an entirely separate area for their "business."

While it may be difficult to look at a little Maltese with hair ribbons or a playful Pug and envision that they think like wolves, the fact is that they do! They all do...regardless of breed, size, or mix of breeds. Most dogs have been domesticated through breeding enough so that they no longer have much of an interest in hunting prey for food (or other more primitive instincts), yet the core instinct of being an inherently clean animal remains.

Additionally, canines are pack animals who view their entire lifestyles based upon pecking order and respect. When leadership is provided, they feel much more comfortable and confident, and find it very easy to follow clearly defined rules.

If leadership is not present, dogs can feel obligated to step into the role of Alpha, a situation that can result in a household leader who has created rules that may be unacceptable to humans.

If the particular dog doesn't have the wherewithal to be the leader, and therefore there is none, this can lead to confusion, lack of confidence, and behavior problems.

Your job as a pet owner is to understand your dog's way of thinking and to use that knowledge to help your dog understand the bathroom rules of your home. This is most easily accomplished by using a technique known as "expanding the den."

Expanding the Den

Because your dog is not a wild animal, but is instead a domesticated pet that resides in your home, you'll need to assist him in creating a mutually acceptable den area for resting, playing, and eating. This will be the first "clean section" where going to the bathroom is not allowed.

In order to accomplish this, you must begin with a small, confined area such as a wire dog crate or the kitchen with gates up. The crate is an extremely valuable tool in many aspects of dog training, which we'll expand upon later. For now, we're covering the concept of expanding the den.

The idea is to provide a safe area that your dog associates with eating and resting. The confinement area should be at least large enough for your dog to stand, sit, lay down and turn around. Anything smaller than that would be uncomfortable and inhumane, anything larger will make house training more difficult and take longer.

Always make a positive association with your dog's den area. Never use the area for punishment, isolation or extremely long periods of time. Your dog should enjoy his area just as a child enjoys having his own room. Your pet will be resting in this location whenever you're not available to personally supervise.

Keeping in mind that your ultimate goal is to have a trustworthy, housebroken dog with free run of the house, the *confinement area should be centrally located in your home*. If you keep your dog (or the crate with the dog in it) in the garage or basement, your dog will become housebroken only in there. You want your pet to be a member of the family who eventually understands that the whole house is the "clean section." While it is not thrilling to have a wire dog crate taking up space in your kitchen, remember it is only temporary.

Following these methods to the letter can have your dog house trained in less than a month! At that point, you may choose to continue with the crate for other reasons, such as preventing chewing, or you may be able to remove it completely.

Most dogs will instinctively keep their confinement area clean. The benefits of this are many. Let's say you're going out for two hours. If your dog is in an area where he doesn't want to eliminate, he will "hold it in" until you get home. Benefit #1: There are no "gifts" on your rug when you return. Benefit #2: As soon as you return home, you will walk your dog and have the opportunity to praise him for going in the right place (outside)! Benefit #3: Your dog is building up muscle control so he can eventually last for the needed periods of time (e.g., a reasonable work day or overnight).

So, how do we *expand* the den? Remember, dogs don't want to soil in the same place where they live! The first place your dog makes that connection with, is the crate or confinement area. Following is the next closest section of your home.

For example, if your dog's crate is in the kitchen, the first clean section (in his mind) will be the crate, followed by the kitchen the crate is in.

Next will be the room of your home where he spends the most time with you. This is usually the family room or living room where you interact with your pet when you are at home.

You'll also be allowing your dog to accompany you to other areas of your home such as your bedroom, bathroom, laundry area, etc. The more time your dog spends in these places (supervised only, and following the rest of the methods of course), the more he will understand that the whole house is the "den," to be kept clean at all times.

By starting with a small area such as a crate, and gradually increasing the area to include your whole home, you'll be expanding the den until your dog feels that *he lives* in the entire house. In his mind, the whole place will soon be the "clean section"!

Dogs are den animals by nature and like to keep their living area clean.

By using a crate for confinement, and gradually expanding from there, your dog will soon realize that your whole home is the "clean section"!

Should You Use a Crate?
Pros, Cons, and How-To's

Pros

By now, just about all people have heard of a crate. It is a wire cage used for confining a dog when you're not available to supervise. Most people are willing to go ahead and use a crate for training because it's highly recommended by all pet professionals. Other people are more resistant. I've often found that even clients who are using a crate still have negative feelings or reservations about the idea.

As we continue through this learning process, I hope you'll become more comfortable with the concept that most dogs actually *enjoy* the crate. Even if I can't bring you that far, hopefully you'll at least become agreeable enough to use one and enjoy all of the associated benefits.

Dogs, being instinctively den animals, enjoy having a space of their own. Particularly in busy households that have children, other pets, or a hectic pace, there is a certain comfort experienced by the dog in having his own private area.

Another characteristic of dogs is that they are pack animals. This means leadership is extremely important to them. The majority of dogs are not "born leaders," and will feel much more comfortable conforming to a clearly defined set of rules.

By consistently using the crate and following an appropriate housebreaking schedule, your dog will feel more confident and comfortable within your family structure.

When consistent leadership is not present, your dog can become confused, anxious, or obligated to step into the position of leader. A confused or anxious dog is not likely to become quickly house trained, and a dog who thinks he's the leader may choose his own desired area for eliminating...and that might not be outside!

In fact, dogs who are the leader of the household may sometimes choose to eliminate in extremely upsetting spots, such as on your couch, bed, or in baby's room! But not to worry...you'll be following the methods detailed in this book and will most certainly not have that problem!

As discussed in Expanding the Den (page 5), using a crate has many associated benefits. It will help your dog learn to "hold it," building up necessary muscle control. When you return home, chances are that your dog will not already have had an accident. Then, when you walk him, you'll have the opportunity to praise him for doing the right thing outside.

Other confinement areas tend to be less effective. For example, your pet is much more likely to have an accident in a whole kitchen than in a properly-sized crate. He would have much less of a feeling of being stuck in a dirty place. While this applies to all dogs, it can be particularly significant in training small breed dogs.

Crate training also helps dog owners have more peace of mind. Particularly if you have a puppy, you will not spend your day worrying about whether or not your dog is urinating, chewing, or doing other inappropriate things while you're out.

Overall, the benefits far outweigh any negatives.

Cons

Are there any downsides to using a crate? Not really.

Some people may resent the crate temporarily taking up space in their kitchen or living room. Others just go with the flow and put a nice houseplant on top of it!

The only other downside is that occasionally a human will use the crate too much. Keep in mind, this pet is a dog, not a hamster. If you work outside the home, your dog should be in the crate only when you are not home, are sleeping, or are in the shower.

Otherwise, even though it's extra work, your dog should be personally supervised by you. While most people are responsible about proper use of the crate, I've occasionally experienced a client who uses it too much.

On those rare occasions, it's usually a very busy household where the dog has already been in the crate the entire work day, where I'll hear, "I just need to put him in for a short time while I _____." (Fill in the blank: cook dinner, give kids a bath, do paper work, get my stuff ready for tomorrow, etc.)

The fact is, pets are extra work and if you aren't up for the supervising, training, vacuuming, and poop-scooping, a dog is probably not the right pet for you.

However, if you put some work into your pet now, you'll soon have a well-behaved dog that is a pleasure to have around. He'll play with the kids while you cook dinner. They'll giggle when he sips water from their bath, and he'll keep you company while you're preparing for tomorrow. (If I figure out how to train dogs to vacuum or scoop poop you'll be one of the first to know!)

If you work an extremely long schedule that results in your dog being crated more than an *absolute maximum* of 8 1/2 hours per day, you'll need to question whether or not a dog is the right pet for you at all. Whether crated or loose, such an overextended period of time is too long to leave a pet home alone with no opportunity to eliminate or socialize. You'll need to either stop home midday, hire a pet-sitter, or consider a new home for the dog.

How-To's

Begin by purchasing a crate that will fit your dog when he is of full size. Even though your dog will be house trained within 30 days, chances are that you'll choose to continue using the crate throughout other training processes (chewing, etc.)

If you have a Labrador Retriever puppy, that could mean several sizes of crates! Instead, purchase a large crate now, including a divider panel that can be used to make it temporarily smaller if necessary. If you are unable to get a divider panel that's made for the crate, a couple of sturdy plastic milk crates will work well too.

Your dog should be able to stand, sit, turn around and lay down comfortably in the crate. It should not be so large that he can do jumping jacks and run around, nor so small as to be cramped.

When you bring the crate into your home, act like it's a great thing! As if this giant box contains the largest dog treat in the world! "Ooooh, Max, look what I've got for you!" Put the crate together in front of your dog and encourage his presence. Let him sniff the pieces and hang out with you while you put it together.

Speaking of putting it together, there will be many types of crates to choose from. I recommend an open, wire type crate, not the travel kind that's plastic with air holes. Remember, your dog is supposed to feel like he's not only in the crate, but also to feel like he's in the *room* that the crate is in.

There will also be choices of folding crates or standard "pin" crates. The folding ones are very convenient, as they set up almost instantly and are folded up quite quickly. If you plan on bringing your dog's crate to other people's homes, on vacation, or moving it around frequently, this is a great choice. They're not quite as sturdy as pin crates but are generally safe and convenient.

A traditional drop-in-pin style crate is usually very sturdy, but more of a process to assemble or disassemble. It's an excellent choice if you plan on basically leaving the crate in one spot, or if your dog has separation anxiety or jumps around in the crate a lot.

Once the crate is assembled, leave the door open and just let your dog hang around it. Open and shut the door a bit so he gets used to the sound. Stick your head inside for a short moment and talk to your dog in a happy voice. Then, sit back and let him have some time to check it out. If he goes inside, praise him but don't shut the door yet.

Next, put a small treat inside the crate and encourage your dog to go in and get it. Some dogs will dive right in, while others may be more tentative. If necessary, you may need to help your dog into the crate to get the treat the first few times. Still don't shut the door yet.

After a few times of this, practice putting your dog inside the crate and shutting the door for just a few seconds. Praise lavishly and let him right out again. Do this about 3 or 4 times and then go about your own activities. Leave the door open and let your dog ponder it on his own a bit.

Most people are shocked at how quickly their dog adapts to the crate. One client of mine, a single woman who had a five year old Maltese with a housebreaking problem was actually crying when I suggested using a crate! She thought her dog would be miserable and sad in there...and it took me four weeks of coming to her (smelly!) apartment for lessons before she finally relented. She set it up, put her dog inside, and her pet actually lay right down and took a nap! Within two days, her dog loved the crate so much he'd go inside and hang out in there even when she was home! By graduation time, her pet was fully house trained but she kept the crate anyway because she didn't have the heart to take it away from him. This is extremely common.

What If My Dog Carries On In the Crate?

Some dogs, especially puppies, may carry on in the beginning, barking and whining because they want you to let them out. It is very important *not* to open the door when your dog is demanding you do. Otherwise you'll be teaching your pet that if he barks, you'll let him out! If you endure 15 minutes of barking until you can't stand it anymore and then give in, you'll only build up his stamina to bark even longer the next time.

Just as babies eventually must learn to sleep through the night without being picked up from their crib, so must your dog learn to relax in the crate for periods of time.

The best way to alleviate this problem is with some obedience training. Obedience commands, such as the "sit," "stay," and "down" will help your dog to understand the meanings of the words "no," and "good dog." Your pet will also learn to respect you more, so when you say "No," he'll feel like he actually has to listen. Some basic commands will be a very important part of the house training process anyway, so be sure to pay attention to the Obedience section later in this book (page 36).

For very young puppies or brand new pets, it can sometimes be helpful to leave a ticking clock nearby, or another white noise, such as a quiet radio set between stations.

Leaving a t-shirt with your scent on it might also help your dog relax a bit, but keep in mind that the shirt might get chewed or dirty.

If your dog carries on in the crate, do not attempt to soothe with a loving voice. Dogs are extremely smart animals, but they think on a much more basic level than humans. If you lay down next to the crate, stroke your pet through the bars and softly say "It's okay, you're a good dog, be quiet," your dog is going to think you're actually saying "Good boy, barking! Good cry in the crate!" *Whenever you use a "praising" voice, your dog is going to feel praised!*

Instead, you need to (in a normal voice) firmly say, "No! No barking! Down and stay!" Then, when your dog is resting nicely, that's when you praise with the nice, soothing voice.

The only times your dog should be removed from the crate while barking is if you've just returned home and he's barking because he's excited to see you. Or, if your dog is a young puppy or an older dog who has never been the slightest bit housebroken, you'll need to use your judgment as to whether he really is barking because he actually needs to do his business.

Genuine need to "go" will be more easily identified if your dog was previously resting quietly and then suddenly starts "asking" to go out.

If you genuinely feel he truly needs to go out (such as in the middle of the night), you'll need to take him in a manner that's strictly business.

Remember, you don't want your dog to feel like he is being rewarded for carrying on in his crate in the middle of the night. If you truly feel he needs a bathroom trip, you'll need to avoid eye contact, bring him directly to the door, clip on his leash, and march straight to the outdoor bathroom area. If he eliminates, provide mild praise, and then walk him right back inside and straight back into the crate.

For a middle of the night "emergency" bathroom trip, there shall be no snuggling, ball playing, or hanging out of any kind. Strictly business, or you'll be doing it forever. Trust me.

> **Be consistent! Remember, *your dog* is not supposed to be training *you!*... You are training your dog!**

Getting Started....
Checklist of Supplies Needed

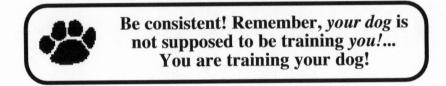

On the following page is a list of all the supplies you'll need to assist you in quickly and more easily house training your dog. You can run out to the stores and get them, or shop for them online.

For the convenience of our clients and readers, I regularly search for the best deals online and have created links on my web site directly to the supplies on the list. Simply visit www.FreeDogTrainingInfo.com and click on "pet supplies" to access some of the best resources for your pet supply needs.

Regardless of where you get them from...just get them. Each and every item on the supply list will be very helpful at some point in the training process. Perhaps the only thing more annoying than your dog having an accident is not having the right cleaner on hand to neutralize the odor.

Check Off Each Item to Make Sure You Have All of Your Supplies On Hand!

☐ **Crate-** Will be used to confine the dog when you're not able to supervise. Be sure to get a wire crate, not a plastic travel type.

☐ **1 or 2 Gates-** As your dog starts to get the hang of things, you'll want to start building up to free run of the house *gradually*. A gate or two will be extremely helpful for keeping your dog in the kitchen, blocking off a hallway, etc.

Consider getting a pressure-mounted gate (no hardware to drill into your walls). Another feature that's really helpful is a gate that has a walk-through section so you don't have to step over it all the time.

If you're putting a gate at the top of a staircase and also have children, you must use a hardware mounted gate...a pressure mounted one is unsafe for kids at the top of steps.

☐ **1 Leash-** For you to personally leash walk your dog to the designated bathroom area outside. Also will be used to walk your dog for socialization and exercise. The best type of leash for training is a leather leash. Next best is a cotton or nylon leash. Do not get a chain leash.

☐ **1 Collar-** Also for you to walk your dog, and for your pet's general safety. Your dog will be wearing his collar at all times...even indoors, so be sure to get one that fits comfortably. It should not be too thick and heavy on your pet's neck, nor should it be thin or flimsy if you have a large dog. For puppies, be sure to get a collar that is size-adjustable so you can readjust it as your dog grows.

☐ **1 Large Bottle of Nature's Miracle Odor Neutralizer Liquid-** It is very important that when your dog has accidents, they are cleaned with an odor neutralizer. Dogs have an extremely strong sense of smell, and will likely return to the same areas for additional accidents if the odor is not neutralized. This product has been very effective on both hard floors and carpets. It's also available in flakes that are special for carpets.

☐ **2 Rolls of Paper Towels-** Yes, you will need them! And if you don't use them all, you can always use them for other things!

☐ **1 20-Foot Long Line-** This is a long, cotton web lead, which should be 20' long, and generally comes in 1/2" width. It is very helpful for several reasons. If you're working on teaching your dog to use a designated area in your yard, after awhile you'll want him to start heading there on his own. By using the long line, you can allow your dog the freedom to go ahead while still having the "insurance" that if he doesn't, you can redirect him to the right spot.

The long line is also extremely helpful if you don't have a fenced yard. Dogs need lots of exercise on a daily basis. From a house training viewpoint, exercise also stimulates dogs to go to the bathroom. By using a long line, you'll be able to let your dog run while still keeping him safe. The long line will also be helpful through various other training exercises such as the "come" command, boundary training, and more.

☐ **A Pooper-Scooper-** Preferably the kind that's like large salad tongs. This allows you to clean up without feeling like you're getting down and dirty.

☐ **Your Housebreaking Chart-** Included in this book! (Page 64).

☐ **A Pencil-** For diligently keeping track of your dog's progress. Be sure to keep the chart and pencil in a convenient location near the door through which your dog is consistently walked.

If you have a yard, you will also need:

☐ **10 to 30 Feet of Inexpensive Garden Border-** If you have a yard and are working toward the goal of having your dog eliminate only in a designated area, this can be very helpful in setting a boundary. A simple, inexpensive wire garden border that you just stick in the ground can help make it clear to your dog which part of the yard is "in" the bathroom area, and which part is "out." The idea is not to fence your pet in...you're simply creating a boundary line.

☐ **A Small Trash Can With a Step-Pop Lid-** This is an excellent item to keep in the designated bathroom area for ease of cleanup. Be sure to choose one where the top overlaps the sides a little, so rain doesn't get in.

Supplies You Will *Not* Need

Wee Wee Pads

A Litter Box

Newspapers

Paper Training

This is a book about house training your dog. In order for your dog to understand that all "business" is to be done outdoors, you will not want to confuse him by also sometimes allowing soiling indoors.

The majority of pet owners see the reasoning behind this, and prefer to simply teach their pet to eliminate outdoors. However, on a regular basis I also receive inquiries from people who want their dog paper trained or litter box trained. My immediate question for those pet owners is, "Why?"

Here are the most common reasons offered:

1) "I work extremely long hours and don't want him to have to hold it in for so long."

2) "I go away on business trips and want to be able to leave the dog home alone for a day or two."

3) "I don't like to go outside in the cold weather and don't want to have to take the dog out."

4) "I don't like to go outside in the hot weather and don't want to have to take the dog out."

5) "I want my dog to stay indoors so he always stays spotlessly clean

and never gets any dirt on him."

6) "I was told by the vet or rescue league not to bring the puppy outdoors until he is completely vaccinated." (A valid point...be sure to read below.)

7) "I am handicapped, and I am physically unable to bring the dog outdoors on a regular basis." (This is the least common answer...be sure to read below.)

When faced with these answers, I find myself faced with both moral and social dilemmas. While I love to make my clients happy, I simply cannot advise that paper training would be appropriate in most of the above situations.

For example, I cringe at the thought of insulting a person by pointing out that dogs are dogs and that they may sometimes get mud on their paws, but at least they'll be housebroken.

However, I also want every client to be happy with the training in the end (no more accidents!), and I feel a responsibility to *all* dogs to ensure their well being. Statistics show that a significant percentage of dogs turned in by their owners to animal shelters are relinquished due to housebreaking and other behavior problems.

My experience has also taught me that those who insist on paper training are also often those who end up with long term house training problems...increasing the likelihood of their dog ending up as a part of the statistics. This is partially because *it is contrary to a dog's natural instincts to eliminate in its home.* It's also very confusing, and overall not conducive to the dog's best interest for dozens of other reasons.

Here are my responses to the above mentioned statements. Please forgive me, as I am forced to set aside my moral and social dilemmas in favor of my client's and their dog's best interests:

#1 & #2- If you are out of the home for such extremely long hours, a dog is probably not the right pet for you. It is inhumane to leave any pet, and particularly a dog, home alone for such extended periods of time. This is not only because of house training issues, but also because of lack of socialization, loneliness, and other potential behavior problems. Dogs are pack animals who require ongoing interaction. Unless you intend to hire a pet sitter to attend to your dog one, two, or three times per day (depending on length of your absence), you should strongly consider re-homing the dog to a more appropriate household.

#3, #4, & #5- If you don't want to go outside, or don't want your pet to go outdoors, a dog is definitely not the right pet for you. You cannot pick and choose on which days your dog should be housebroken and on which days you prefer paper training. Further, lack of socialization and not enough exercise are both problems that are guaranteed to occur under these circumstances. A dog who is not properly socialized and who doesn't get enough exercise is likely to develop aggression problems, fear problems, excessive barking, chewing, obesity, and a plethora of others. If you want a pet who always stays indoors, is spotlessly clean, and doesn't need to be walked, I would honestly recommend a nice house cat instead of a dog. They are truly wonderful pets and can meet all the criteria in statements 3, 4, & 5.

#6- Almost every pet owner who purchases or adopts a puppy is advised by their vet or rescue league that their puppy should not be brought outdoors until all vaccinations are completed. There are many diseases that can be contracted outdoors via airborne viruses, or even picked up from the urine of a squirrel that hopped by earlier that day. This is the reason for vaccinating our pets in the first place.

When I first became a dog trainer, (10+ years prior to writing this book), I noticed a big problem...people were waiting until their puppies were completely finished will *all* of the vaccines and boosters before bringing their puppies outside! In most cases, this meant that the puppy had not left the house until 4 - 5 months of age.

During that time, scads of newspapers were used for the puppies' soiling indoors, the client's homes were filled with stains and odors, and the pets were lacking in socialization.

I asked myself this question: "Which is worse...the potential exposure to diseases, or the almost definite likelihood of developing long term housebreaking problems?" Wanting to be sure my instincts were correct, and holding my responsibility to my clients in the highest regard, I decided to consult with some veterinarians for their opinions. I personally met with five different veterinarians from different animal hospitals, without advising them of each others' answer. And do you know what every one of them told me? Following is the summary:

<u>Summary of Veterinarian Interviews</u>
Regarding Paper Training vs.
House Training of Young Puppies

All of the veterinarians interviewed expressed that, in their professional opinions, *the risk of developing a serious housebreaking problem was more hazardous* than the likelihood of contracting a disease in the dog's own backyard.

Since puppies are given their first round of immunizations before they ever leave their litter, they felt that if prudence and caution were exercised, it would be better to house train the puppy right away and skip the paper training altogether.

Every doctor expressed that they personally did not paper train their own pups at all! They trained them for outdoor eliminating, and practiced extreme caution by limiting exposure to the elements.

Each veterinarian stressed that the puppy should be brought only from the door of the house to one spot on the property for the purpose of eliminating. The puppy is not to be permitted to roam free, eat sticks, or otherwise receive exposure to potentially harmful germs until the vaccines are complete.

Of course, there may be a veterinarian reading this book who disagrees. I'm certain that there's no opinion in the world that every person will agree on straight across the board.

There are also a few exceptions, as in a rescue person who is hand feeding pups that are extremely young, and do not have the benefit of their mother's milk or first shots.

In over 10 years of training dogs, not once have I ever had a client whose puppy contracted a disease from the limited outdoor exposure of house training.

Hence, skip the paper training!

Special Section on Paper Training For the Disabled

#7- For those who are truly handicapped, paper training might be the right solution. However, when I speak of a handicap, I do not mean "I occasionally have a stiff knee due to surgery I had three years ago." I also don't mean "I'm too tired," or "I purchased a dog that's too powerful and disobedient to be walked."

If you are a truly disabled person who honestly feels there is no other way for your dog's bathroom schedule to be met, do not despair. Every technique in this book still applies to your dog.

You will still need to use a clean confinement area, work with the expanding the den concept, and follow all the methods in this book to the letter. The only difference will be that every time I refer to walking your dog to the designated area outdoors, you will instead bring your dog to the designated area indoors.

Having read the section on Expanding the Den (page 5), you'll realize that paper training will be much more easily accomplished if you do not locate the papers (designated bathroom area) in a central part of the home. Dogs, being innately clean animals, will not want to use the papers if, for example, they're located in the kitchen. The bathroom area needs to be as far as possible from the dog's main living space...perhaps way down the hall in the laundry room, or out in the garage.

Of course, you also will not use the "bathroom" area for confinement...otherwise your dog will think of it as "home" and will not want to eliminate there! *Remember, you're following all of the methods in this book to the letter, with the exception that your dog's designated area is on papers in a "not part of the dog's living space" part of your home.*

For ease of cleanup, many clients have found it helpful to purchase an extra crate tray (the tray that's normally in the bottom of a wire crate). Of course, your dog will still need the tray that's in his crate, so you'll need to get an extra one. By keeping the newspapers or wee wee pads on the tray, the urine will not "run off" and spread along the whole floor. The tray will also help provide a clear boundary for your pet as to where is "in" the bathroom, and where is not.

If your disability dictates that paper training is the only way to address your dog's elimination needs, please remember that socialization is also extremely important. Even if you can't work with the daily in/out, in/out of outdoor housebreaking, it is still important to get your dog out of the house to be socialized with the world. Invite visitors over. Take a jaunt around the neighborhood whenever possible, and bring along the dog. If you have special needs, you may need to work with a professional trainer to teach your pet how to walk with you, but the benefits to both of you will be worth it!

Designated Bathroom Area
Reasons, Consistency, & Selecting a Spot

Consistency is the key to house training your pet. Dogs are creatures of habit (aren't we all?)...and will quickly fall into the routine you create for them. You will need to consistently feed, give water, and walk your dog at the same times each day.

By walking your dog to a designated area outside, you will reap many benefits. The first is obvious...your dog will learn to eliminate in one area instead of all over your property.

Less obvious is the fact that the area will quickly become a "trigger." Every time you bring your dog to that spot, he will go if he has to. In fact, most dogs will at least squeeze out a few drops simply because of the subconscious need associated with the area, combined with the desire to receive your praise.

This can be extremely convenient when it's time to leave for work and you need to make sure your dog "goes," or for example, when a thunderstorm is in the process of rolling in. As soon as your dog reaches that spot he or she will at least try.

Begin by selecting your designated area. If you have a yard, choose an area that's far enough from your patio that it won't hinder your enjoyment of your yard. It should be a corner that provides your dog with some privacy, yet is also not in the walking path used to enter/exit your yard.

If you have a very large yard, also avoid choosing an area that's extremely far from your door or involves trampling through the forest to get there. Don't forget...your dog will be going out there at all times of the day and evening, and so will you!

The minimum size of the designated area should be no smaller than approximately 4 x 7 feet. If you have multiple dogs, it will need to be larger.

You can just leave the grass that's already there, or consider putting down gravel or rocks. Concrete, wood chips, wood decking, etc., are not recommended...partially because your dog's natural instincts are not going to be as strong on concrete, and partially because wood will hold odors and bacteria and be difficult to keep sanitary.

Always choose a designated area that's going to be the permanent one. The tactic of using a spot right outside your door because it's winter, with the plan of moving it in the spring will backfire. You will end up with a dog who still soils right outside the door even in summer. And he'd be right because that's what you taught him!

If you live in a climate where there is likely to be snow to deal with, you'll just have to tough it out and plan on shoveling a path to the acceptable permanent area...and plan on doing it every winter, even after your dog is trained! Remember, if you don't want to wade through waist-high snow to get there (or leaves, sticks, or whatever), neither will your dog!

Another thing that is helpful, is to section off the area using a short, wire garden border. This can help your dog to more clearly recognize which part is "in" the bathroom, and which part is "out." The idea is simply to provide a boundary line, not to fence your dog in. It's also great for people who have children because it helps kids remember not to run through there.

For Apartment Dwellers....Choosing a Designated Area

Even if you live in an apartment, a designated area is an important key to house training your dog. As discussed above, you want to create a "trigger" spot that your dog will immediately recognize as the place to "go." Choose a particular bush, tree, or fire hydrant that you'll use as the consistent spot.

If you live in an apartment building, keep in mind the distance your dog has to travel down the stairs or elevator, and through the lobby to get outside. While you may not choose the flowers immediately outside the front door, be realistic by also not choosing a tree two blocks away.

For Avid Lawn Lovers

Occasionally I've come across a client who has a yard but doesn't want the dog to eliminate there at all. "If I don't mind leash walking him around the neighborhood, then it should be fine." This is true. You can always personally leash walk your dog off your property for eliminating, thereby planning on keeping every inch of your lawn absolutely perfect.

But keep in mind, there will be other times when your dog has access to your yard.

For example, let's say you're having a family cookout. If your dog spends two or three hours in the yard enjoying the party, chances are that he'll need to "go" at some point. And your yard *is outdoors*, (therefore, you'd never correct your dog for eliminating outside in the yard). If your dog has not been trained to use a designated bathroom area, he may choose to urinate smack in the middle of the grass instead of off in a corner!

By teaching your dog to use a designated spot, it can serve as the lesser of two evils. Once your dog is completely trained, you might choose to mostly go on leash walks for eliminating. But on the occasion when he *is* in the yard, using the designated area will be highly preferable to your prized rose bushes!

Upkeep Of the Designated Area

One of the very important things to keep in mind regarding house training, is that dogs are innately clean animals. This means that if the designated area is dirty, they will not want to go there! You should never allow more than one or two "land mines" to accumulate in the area...which means it's got to be cleaned up every single day.

A very simple and easy way to keep up with this is as follows: get a small plastic or stainless steel trash can with one of those step-pop lids. Make sure to choose one where the lid overlaps the sides a little so rain won't get inside. Keep this trash can, lined with a double layer of kitchen trash bags, inside or next to the designated bathroom area.

Also get a pooper-scooper...but not just any scooper. Get the kind that's like giant salad tongs, and also keep it conveniently next to the little garbage can at the designated area.

The reason for these supplies is because...let's face it...the poop scooping aspect is not one of the best parts of pet ownership. In fact, it's a pretty poopy kind of job that most people avoid like the plague.

If your system of cleanup is to use a little shovel and scoop it into an open pail, it can be a job that can truly make you want to gag! Ditto if you use plastic bags each time or some other down and dirty method.

The long handled, salad tong-style poop-scooper keeps you standing up...far away from the actual poop! You simply open the tongs and shut them around the pile. Then, use your foot to step on the pedal of the garbage pail, it flips open, and you drop the odoriferous pile inside. Viola. Done. You can even do this in a cocktail dress or a business suit. No need to get on your knees, smell anything, or touch anything! Much easier to keep up with on a daily basis. Trust me.

As for the urinating, you can keep odors at bay by rinsing the area with water on a regular basis. If it hasn't rained in awhile, you may need to rinse it down with a hose. Approximately once every two to four weeks (depending on dog size, # of dogs, etc.), you can sanitize the area by using a kennel cleaning solution, or good old bleach and water. Both can be easily applied using one of those garden sprayers that are very inexpensive, easy to use, and attach to the end of a garden hose.

For easy access to all of the needed pet and garden supplies, I have searched out the best prices and created convenient lists that bring you directly to the items. Simply visit my web site at www.FreeDogTrainingInfo.com and click on "pet supplies."

Using a designated bathroom area has many advantages.

Your dog will know exactly why he's being walked there, and your yard will stay cleaner and nicer.

Whether a private homeowner or an apartment dweller, every dog owner can benefit from using a designated area.

Choosing & Using a Trigger Phrase

Another helpful element in training your dog to eliminate outside is to use a "trigger" phrase that your dog will recognize as the command for going to the bathroom. Initially, you'll always walk your dog to the designated bathroom area. But you also don't want him to think that he can only go there!

By having your dog recognize a phrase, he'll much more easily understand what you mean when you want him to do his business at another location, such as when you're visiting someone else's home, before entering the vet or groomer's office, or if you're on vacation.

Most people choose one of the following phrases: "Do your business," "Go make," "Hurry up," or "Go potty." Of course, you can choose whatever phrase comes naturally to you. Just make sure you choose one phrase and stick with it permanently. All family members should agree on the phrase and should consistently use it every single time.

There are three main scenarios in which you'll use the phrase:

1) Use the phrase every time you walk your dog to the designated area,

stated as a command in a normal, matter-of-fact, friendly voice. "Do your business!"

2) Use the phrase as a part of praising your dog. While he's physically "going," very *calmly* and quietly say, "Good boy do your business, good." When he's just finished going, very excitedly and playfully exclaim, "Good boy! Good do your business! Good boy!"

3) When you want your dog to eliminate in a spot other than the designated area, such as immediately before entering the groomer's shop, choose an appropriate spot and use the phrase then too. It will help your dog to understand what you want him to do.

Consistently using the trigger phrase is very important. I've occasionally worked with clients who did not make sure their dog recognizes a phrase. They were then faced with a problem where their dog was so thoroughly geared for the designated area that he would hold it in all day and wait to return home to the spot before eliminating.

Others have taken their dog on vacation and have been plagued with spending three hours walking the dog because he was holding back for the same reason. This can easily be avoided by using the trigger phrase. And it's an important part of the housebreaking process anyway. So go ahead and choose one. You may feel silly at first, but that's part of the fun of being a dog owner. You get to be silly!

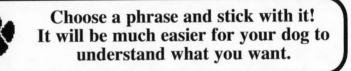

Choose a phrase and stick with it! It will be much easier for your dog to understand what you want.

Your Mindset

One of the most important parts of house training your dog will be your way of thinking. In the Introduction to this book, I said your dog will be housebroken in 30 days or less. I did not say it was going to be easy or relaxing. In fact, it will involve considerable effort on your part in following the schedule, personally leash walking your dog, and supervising constantly.

However, the good news is that with diligence, your dog will truly be 100% house trained and trustworthy. You will not spend the next several months or years cleaning up accidents, replacing carpets, and being embarrassed by your pet. It will be over with quickly, and then you can continue on with the business of enjoying your dog!

There's an old adage that says, "Old habits die hard." This is true in many aspects of life, and your habits with your dog are no exception. There may be some things that you've always done a certain way. Some of them may be different than what I'm recommending in this book.

Let go.

Instead of fighting change, and insisting on holding on to old ways of doing things, keep yourself open to vigilantly following the advice in this book. I can write the book. You can buy it. But you will not reap the benefits if you don't follow the methods. Here's to change!

Special Section For Older Dogs

"You can't teach an old dog new tricks."

"My dog is different."

"You don't understand, I've already tried x, y, & z with my dog."

"He'll never change."

These are common phrases often declared by frustrated owners of adult dogs who have had ongoing house training problems...possibly for years.

As of the writing of this book, I have been a Certified Master Dog Trainer for over 10 years, specializing in family pets. I've trained hundreds of dogs of all ages (with house training issues) most of whom have become 100% housebroken.

In those rare instances when the pet has not become 100% house trained, it was due to the inconsistency of the owners, their resistance to following the methods, or their (forgive me!) laziness in not following the schedule. Never once was it because the dog couldn't learn, their pet was "different" or any of the other available excuses.

In fact, my oldest graduates that had housebreaking problems solved were 10 and 11 years old! They were two little Chihuahuas who had a territory marking competition going on for years. The owner was not happy about it, but apparently was not bothered enough to do anything about it...until she became pregnant. Suddenly the thought of a baby crawling around in a house that had little squirts of urine all over was not very appealing!

Within two weeks of starting the training, the problem was under control. By the end of the training program, the dogs were 100% housebroken, using a designated area outside, and had free run of the house.

Literally hundreds of our clients' adult or senior dogs, who have had confusion for years, are now house trained and trustworthy. If they can do it, so can you and your dog.

The average life expectancy of a dog is 15 years. If you have a seven year old dog with a house training problem, why declare, "It's too late"? By teaching him now, you could save yourself potentially eight more years of cleaning up accidents, enduring odors, and feeling resentful toward your pet!

Occasionally I come across a client who has an older dog who was previously house trained and has suddenly regressed. Often, the dog has the owner convinced that he is now incontinent and simply cannot hold it.

In these cases, I recommend a veterinary checkup to see if that's the case. Almost 100% of the time, the vet finds that there is nothing physically wrong with the dog.

In many of these cases, the accidents are a symptom of the dog either being lazy or dominating the owner. As with all other house training issues, these pets come around very nicely with some obedience, personal leash walking, supervision, food and water scheduling, etc.

In the rare case when a veterinarian does discover a physical incontinence, following a house training schedule can still be very helpful. After all, what goes in must come out, right? By following a feeding, watering, and walking schedule, you can at least help an elderly, incontinent dog cut down on the number of accidents.

In short, house training your pet will be much more easily accomplished if you set your mind to it. Plan to change old habits. Don't let your dog pull the wool over your eyes. And soon, you too will be enjoying a trustworthy pet!

Feeding Your Pet

Feeding Schedule

Feeding your pet properly can be a significant key to preventing or alleviating many behavior problems, not the least of which is housebreaking. Very simply stated, "What goes in must come out!"

However, as with most simple statements, there are many other factors to consider. One being that *what* you put in will determine what comes out. Also, knowing *when* it went in will help estimate when it will come out.

That said, your dog will need to eat meals at scheduled times. You will leave the food down for 20 minutes, giving him ample opportunity to eat. *At the end of 20 minutes, you will pick up the dish, and your dog is not to be fed again until the next scheduled meal time.* Obviously if he's standing at the dish still eating, allow a few more minutes to finish...although most dogs gobble their meal in two minutes flat!

Choose the appropriate # of meals per day from the chart below*

Age of Dog	Daily # of Meals
Up to 12 Weeks	4 Meals Per Day
12 Weeks to 6 Months	3 Meals Per Day
6 Months to 1 Year	2 Meals Per Day
1 Year or Older	1 or 2 Meals Per Day**

*Keep in mind, these recommendations are *averages* for all dogs. If you have a medium-sized breed, chances are that these exact recommendations will be perfect. However, if you have a teacup poodle, it's likely that by five months of age he won't be hungry enough to eat three meals a day. Likewise, if you have a giant breed, like a Newfoundland, you'll need to continue the multiple feedings much longer.

**Most adult dogs are fine with eating just one meal per day, in the morning. However, in some cases owners may choose to feed two smaller meals per day permanently. Some reasons would include: you enjoy feeding him twice a day, your dog seems very hungry all the time, or he eats so fast, he ends up regurgitating the meal. In these cases, two smaller meals per day permanently are fine.

For Those Who Currently Leave
Their Dog's Food Out All Day

There are many people who leave their dog's food out all day. The most common reason is:

"My dog is a finicky eater and hardly touches his food, so I leave it out hoping he'll eat more."

I've also heard many other excuses, including hoping he'll digest better, not being available to feed him at the same times every day, he's too skinny, or it's just easier.

There are many problems with leaving your dog's food out all day.

One is that food which sits out all day is likely to collect bacteria, dust, insects, or other disgustingness.

Another is that many dogs will become possessive of the food dish area, and may display territorial behavior...even when they're not currently eating. Not coincidentally, these are often the same dogs that are the "finicky" eaters...they're really not as interested in eating the food...they're more interested in guarding it.

Third, and (since this is a house training book) most important, is that leaving your dog's food out is extremely non-conducive to becoming reliably housebroken! In order to keep track of your dog's elimination schedule, it's very important to know exactly *when* he ate.

"But I'm afraid my dog will practically starve if I don't leave the food out all day. You don't understand...if I leave the food down for only 20 minutes, he'll eat nothing!"

Did you ever cook a Thanksgiving dinner at your house? Or any other kind of a big party or feast? All day, you cook and taste, cook and taste. You eat dozens of tiny tidbits all day. By the time you actually serve the dinner, you're not even hungry! The same is true for your dog.

Remember, you purchased this book so your dog can become thoroughly house trained. 100% house trained! That means old habits will have to go. It will take some willpower on your part, but I guarantee that after one or two missed meals, your dog will be hungry and will eat!

Let's say your dog is going to be on a twice a day feeding schedule. Let's say you've chosen 8 am and 6 pm. At 8 am, you'll give your dog his food. He may not eat it. At 8:20 am you'll call him to the dish "Come Max!" and show him the food. He may turn his face away and not eat. You now know with confidence that you've given him every opportunity to eat and he must currently not be hungry. You will pick up the dish and put it away.

During the day, there will be no snacks, treats, people food, or dog food of any kind.

At 6 pm you'll feed him again. Chances are that he will be hungry, but let's assume he's not. Again, you'll leave the dish for 20 minutes, call him for one more chance, then remove the dish and put it away.

The next morning at 8 am when you feed your dog, he will gobble it up like you've never seen a dog eat before! You will know, in your heart of hearts, that there is nothing wrong with your dog's appetite, and he's been pulling the wool over your eyes all this time. It is certain that if not at 8 am, he will definitely be ravenous by 6 pm.

Try it. It actually will work, and you'll be on track permanently.

Feeding Your Pet: A Proper Diet

When feeding your dog or puppy, it's important to feed the right kind of food. Giving your dog table scraps between meals, tons of treats all day, or high quantities of wet food are all practices that are not conducive to house training.

If you have a very young puppy under the age of 12 weeks, you will need to feed wet puppy food for ease of chewing. You should also introduce dry kibble little by little. If your puppy seems to have a hard time chewing it, you can soften the dry food by soaking it in a little warm water.

If your puppy is between 12 and 16 weeks, you may choose to still use *some* wet puppy food, also for ease of chewing. However, you should be gradually increasing dry kibble so your dog is moving toward a diet of dry food alone.

For adult dogs and puppies over 16 weeks, a diet of only dry food is recommended. This is because it's generally much healthier, as wet dog food tends to contain unnecessary amounts of fats, sugar, sodium, and byproducts. From a housebreaking viewpoint, the more "waste" in the food, the more waste from the dog! Wet food can cause stools to be much softer, more frequent, and more difficult to track.

When choosing an appropriate dry dog food, most experts agree that just about any premium brand of food is acceptable. Pay attention to the formulas they now come in.

For example, a fully grown dog should not still be eating a puppy formula. A puppy should not be eating an adult formula. And much older dogs can definitely benefit from the new senior formulas as well. Choosing the right food will contribute to your dog's health, well-being, and will be best for housebreaking.

Remember the number of meals chart above? Just as the correct number of meals can fluctuate from dog to dog, remember that changing your pet's food formula will be specific to your dog's breed and size as well. Use your best judgment or consult with your veterinarian to decide when is the best time to change to an adult or senior formula.

If or when you do switch your dog's food, be sure to change it gradually, over the course of 10 days. On the first day, just add a bit of the new food to the old. Little by little increase the new food and reduce the old, until it's completely changed. This will help your dog adjust to his new diet without stomach upset.

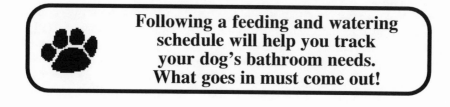

Following a feeding and watering schedule will help you track your dog's bathroom needs. What goes in must come out!

Water

Water is one of the most commonly misconceived topics when it comes to house training. Dogs, like all living things, need lots of water to be healthy and to keep digestive processes going smoothly.

Many people mistakenly think they should limit their dog's water during housebreaking. Not so! But while your dog's water intake should not be *limited*, it does need to be *tracked*. This means that your pet should drink lots of water throughout the day.

However, instead of simply filling the bowl and leaving it on the floor, you'll need to keep the bowl up on your counter.

When offering your dog some water, fill the bowl with fresh water while making a big deal. "Oooh, Buddy look! Water!" When you put the bowl down, you can also use a phrase such as, "Drink water," and praise "Good boy, drink water!"

You may be surprised that your dog will actually drink more water using this method than he would when the bowl is left available all day. The big benefit for training is that now you know exactly *when* he drank it! And what goes in must come out. You'll know that if your dog drank half a bowl of water, he'll need to urinate soon...probably within 10 minutes.

Therefore, you'll also know that this is not the time to allow free run of the living room, and that he'll need to be walked to the designated area very soon.

Keep in mind that if you're going to bed at 11 pm, last water should be given at 10. By giving the water one hour before turning in, you'll be able to give your dog ample opportunity to urinate at "last time out," and you'll be able to go to sleep knowing you're tucking in an "empty" pet.

Have you ever gone on a long road trip? What does everyone do before hitting the road? They go to the bathroom! Or at least try. I'll try not to be too graphic, but did you ever notice that if you really didn't have to go, but you just tried anyway...next thing you know, you're on the freeway and need to use the bathroom only half an hour later? I've noticed the same thing with dogs. If they urinate when they have a very full bladder, then they tend to completely empty themselves. This is something to keep in mind when tracking water before work, sleep, etc.

Supervision

Read this section, and then read it again. I cannot stress to you enough how important it is to supervise your dog constantly throughout the house training process!

Your #1 task in teaching your dog is to make sure you are personally there every single time your dog eliminates. This means that if your dog urinates or defecates outside, you need to personally be there to praise lavishly, "Good boy, do your business, good boy!" It also means that if your dog has an accident indoors, you need to personally catch him in the act and correct him, "No, no, no, no!"

Dogs are very intelligent animals. However, they also have very short attention spans. If your dog already pooped in the yard, and you wait until he comes to the back door to praise him, he thinks you're praising him for coming to the door...not for pooping!

Likewise, if your dog urinated on the rug 10 seconds ago, and is now walking down the hall, if you correct him, he'll think you're correcting him for walking down the hall! (Even if you drag him over and show it to him.)

You must catch your dog *in the act* in order for your praise or correction to be understood correctly. Timing is everything.

Okay, now go back and read this section again. Go on...I'm not kidding!

> ### Supervision is perhaps *the most important* key in house training your pet!
>
> ### You must be <u>personally present</u> to praise or correct...every single time your dog eliminates!

More on Supervision

I'm certain that after reading it twice, you must understand how important it is to supervise your dog constantly during the house training process. But you also may be thinking that's easier said than done! After all, everyone has other responsibilities to take care of around their home, including answering the phone, household chores, taking a shower, preparing meals, or maybe caring for kids. And without a doubt, a multitude of other things too.

With a little creativity, you can find ways to include your dog in many of the day-to-day activities around your home. For example, when preparing a meal, bring your dog's toys into the kitchen and put up your gate so he stays in. Then, while cooking, keep a peripheral eye on your pet so you know what he's doing.

If you're sitting in your office doing some paperwork or paying bills, bring your dog's toys in with you and shut the door so he can't leave.

If you're in a large room, such as a great room, den, or living room that has no way of being gated, remember that your dog's leash can be used indoors too! Keep him by your side while reading the kids a bedtime story.

These suggestions will also help with creating a bond between you, your dog, and other family members. Remember the section on

Expanding the Den? These ideas will help with that too. You want your dog to feel like he lives in the *whole* house...not just his crate or the kitchen.

But what about other times, like when you're in the shower? Remember, your dog's crate does not have to be used only for longer periods of time. It can be used for short times too. Even just for 15 minutes while you're in the shower, or for two minutes while you run the trash to the outside pail.

With a little creativity, and a ban on laziness, you can find ways to include supervising your dog in almost every activity or chore around your home. And when it starts to get you down, remember, it's only temporary! The more diligently you follow the methods, the more quickly your dog will be trustworthy. Your dog will become dependable, and for the rest of his years, you'll enjoy the best possible relationship with your pet.

Exercise and Its Role in House Training

For all living things, exercise is important for keeping digestive systems running smoothly. Making sure your dog gets exercise on a regular basis is a significant factor in house training your dog. In fact, many dogs will instinctively do a fast track around the house or yard, a couple of figure 8's and a loop-the-loop immediately before defecating.

Let's say you're pretty sure your dog needs to eliminate, but just doesn't seem to be getting the urge, or is very distracted. You can try using a little exercise to get things going.

Run back and forth with your dog on a leash, or play a little ball. Consider using your 20' long line to allow your pet to "run free" while still having some control to reign him in.

As soon as the exercise stops, be sure to re-enter the designated bathroom area so that hopefully he ends up going in the desired spot. Praise lavishly. Remember, if he goes in a different spot outside, never correct...it is still outdoors!

Keep in mind that dogs should not be *strenuously* exercised immediately after eating a meal or drinking large quantities of water.

There is a medical condition that can occur, called Gastric Torsion or Bloat. Although it is rather rare, it can be a serious, even fatal condition. More common in deep chested breeds, basically what it usually involves is a "sloshy belly." If a dog exercises extensively with a very full stomach, this could potentially result in a flipping of the stomach, causing digestive processes to shut down. It is not something you need to be in a panic about...just aware of.

As a general rule, I recommend waiting 45 minutes after a full meal before rigorously exercising a dog. When giving water during play, offer small amounts at a time rather than allowing your dog to guzzle an entire bucket in one slurp. Your dog should be safe if you follow these guidelines.

Exercise can help stimulate your dog to "do his business!"

Spaying & Neutering

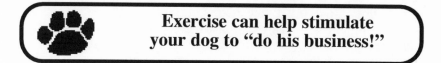

Most people are familiar with the recommendations of all pet professionals to have their dogs spayed or neutered. Spaying is for females. Neutering is for males. This simple surgical procedure prevents dogs from procreating, and can also drastically reduce their instincts to mark their territory, run away, or perform a plethora of other unwanted behaviors.

Have you ever met a vet, groomer, dog trainer, rescue person, or any other pet professional that doesn't recommend spaying and neutering? Unless you are a professional breeder with a particularly strong breeding stock, or an avid competitor in show, chances are the answer is "no".

There are many reasons why spaying and neutering are so strongly recommended. There are medical, behavioral, and pet overpopulation reasons. The explanations are so abundant that I could write another entire book about them! But since this is a book about house training, I'll focus on the housebreaking reasons.

Both male and female dogs have the instinct to mark their territory. Although the tendency is stronger in males, females have the instinct too. Males often make their marking even more prevalent with their leg lifting strategies, although I have seen many females that will practically do a handstand to get their scent where they want it to be.

Altering your pet can significantly reduce the likelihood of territorial marking indoors and out. Leg lifting along the furniture, in the baby's room, or on the garbage pail can be a serious problem. Households that have other pets, or homes that have undergone a big change in lifestyle (such as a new job or a new baby), are also much more likely to experience marking problems if their dog is not spayed or neutered. In fact, I've seen numerous cases in multiple dog households where both dogs are doing it, like a competition!

Spaying and neutering can also help you train your dog to use only the designated area in your yard. The reduced urge to mark his territory can minimize the amount of urinating in other sections. If you're an avid gardener who doesn't wish for your dog to urinate on your prized roses, altering your pet can be helpful.

However, keep in mind that it will not completely eliminate your pet's natural instinct to mark. He is still a dog. Chances are that if some squirrel has been hanging out near a rose bush, your dog may still want to mark there anyway. In these cases, you have to just realize that your dog *is* an animal and that, like many other things in life, you have to "take the bad with the good."

It's possible that if you have one or two special sections outdoors where you really don't want him to go, you may be able to correct the behavior and redirect to the designated area. However, I would strongly recommend against this until at least 6 months to 1 year *after* your dog is 100% house trained. It would have to be done very carefully, with precise supervision and timing, hand in hand with personally leash walking and praising in the designated area. Again, this is not a top priority until all confusions have long been ironed out.

The general recommendation for spaying and neutering is at six months of age. Of course, if your dog is already three years old, you can still have him altered. The myths that females should always have one heat first, or that males won't be as good watchdogs are exactly that...myths.

Spaying and neutering are best for your dog, your family, and the entire canine race. So if you haven't already done so, please contact your vet for an appointment immediately. I thank you, your dog thanks you, and your furniture thanks you too.

Obedience Makes
a Huge Difference

Obedience training can have a *huge* impact on your success in house training your dog. I'm not talking about turning your dog into a circus dog or a show dog, just a well-behaved pet.

Basic obedience commands, such as "heel" (walk at my side), "sit," "down," "stay" and "come," should be a part of every dog's life. These commands will strongly contribute to housebreaking your pet, and they will also help avoid numerous other behavior problems.

Basic manners, such as no jumping, biting, chewing, running away, and more, are also beneficial for a strong foundation of respect between you and your dog.

Many people reading this book will think to themselves, "I really don't care about that other stuff...I just want the dog to be house trained!"

Understandable. But if you read the remainder of this section, you'll understand how obedience ties into house training your pet, and into every other behavior for that matter.

<u>Obedience = Housebreaking</u>
Seven Important Factors

1) When you work on basic obedience commands with your dog, he'll much more clearly understand the meanings of "no" and "good boy". Then, when you use "no" and "good boy" with the house training, he'll much more clearly understand what you mean.

2) Your dog will also respect you more. If you earn your dog's respect by being consistent with obedience commands, he'll feel more like it's <u>not okay</u> to soil in *your* territory...your territory being the entire house.

3) If your dog respects you, he will more likely follow your rules, one of which is no eliminating in the house!

4) Obedience and manners training will help your dog to have more self-control. This can make a vast difference when it comes to every aspect of housebreaking. Particularly if you have a dog with a submissive or excitement urinating problem, it is imperative that you work on obedience commands.

5) Obedience also increases your dog's attention span. Have you ever tried to bring a puppy out to go to the bathroom on a beautiful spring day? Between the birds chirping, squirrels scampering, and irresistible scents in the air, it can seem impossible to get your dog to focus on the business at hand. Obedience training will help him focus.

6) Working on some basic commands can also help your dog to mature a bit. And mature dogs especially do not like to soil where they live.

7) A learning curve is very important in any teaching environment. Why do you think toddlers go to preschool? It's so they can learn *how* to learn. By working on commands, your dog will recognize a "learning environment" in your body language and eye contact. Then, when you use your teaching body language during house training, he'll catch on more easily.

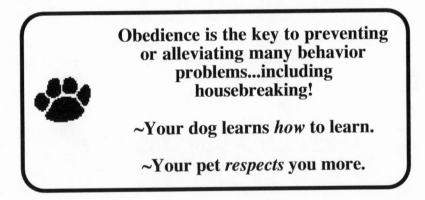

Obedience is the key to preventing or alleviating many behavior problems...including housebreaking!

~Your dog learns *how* to learn.

~Your pet *respects* you more.

Choosing a Dog Trainer

If you don't have any experience working on obedience commands, it will be best to work with a professional dog trainer. Even those who are experienced dog owners can benefit. There's always more to learn, and it can help to know someone is checking to make sure you're practicing regularly!

When choosing a trainer, you'll be faced with many options. The first decision is whether to go with a group class or private training.

When you attend a group class, the trainer's attention will be divided between the many dogs in the class. Group trainers may not be able to take a lot of time out to answer very specific questions, or to customize methods for each dog's individual personality. Group classes can however, be excellent for socialization, or for more experienced dogs to practice in very high distraction environments.

Private training can be excellent in that you have the trainer's undivided attention and the trainer has plenty of time to answer specific questions. Methods should be customized for your own dog's personality. This can be a bit more costly option, but it is often a significant savings compared to the costs that can be incurred by having a dog with behavior problems.

Whatever you decide, you'll want to find out who the trainer is, what their education is, how much experience they have, and what methods they'll be using. Contacting your veterinarian can be an excellent source for a referral to a local, reputable trainer.

When considering training methods, be sure to contemplate what they are, and what you feel comfortable with. There are an extremely wide variety of training methods available, which would require another entire book to describe in detail.

To summarize, you'll need to decide whether you want your dog to wear a head halter paired with treats, wear a traditional collar paired with constant treats, or use a traditional collar reinforced with praise, correction, and perhaps occasional treats. Any methods that involve physical punishment, yelping dogs, or anything else harmful, should immediately be disqualified.

After careful consideration, an in-depth education as a Certified Master Dog Trainer, and over 10 years of experience, I prefer a balance of positive and negative reinforcement. The positive reinforcement being lavish praise, a tone of fun for the dog, and occasional treats. The negative reinforcement being a corrective tug of the leash or collar.

My professional opinion is that dogs instinctively, in a pack environment, do not "bribe" one another into listening. If a subordinate dog within the pack approaches the Alpha while eating, he or she does not give it a piece of food to get it to go away. Rather, a corrective growl or snap is given.

Likewise, I don't feel I should have to be armed with a piece of cheese in order for my pet to come when called. He should come because he respects me, as I've earned his respect through consistency, lavish praise, fun training, and fair correction.

If you live in the Raleigh, NC area, you can contact my company directly, at www.BestPawOnline.com for more information on training.

Praise & Correction

Praise

Building upon the previous chapters, you're probably catching on that your dog is to be supervised constantly, personally leash walked to the designated area for eliminating, and praised for doing so.

Every single time your dog urinates or defecates outside, you will need to praise your dog lavishly. Ideally, you'll praise twice for each time he goes. First, while he's actually in the process, and then immediately when finished.

Whenever your praise your dog, be sure to include your trigger phrase in the praise. "Good boy, do your business, good boy!"

When praising your dog while still in the process of eliminating, be sure to praise calmly and quietly. Don't pet him at this point, otherwise you may interrupt him and he may not finish. For very excitable dogs or puppies, you might need to avoid eye contact to prevent getting him excited and distracted.

When praising your dog immediately after he's finished, that's when you praise very excitedly, bring out the marching band, etc. "Good boy!!! Do your business!!! Good!!!" Feel free to pet, play with, and get your dog all happy and riled up. Maybe toss the ball a little, and really whoop it up.

Also, if your dog urinates or defecates outdoors but not in the designated area, you must NEVER correct him! After all, it is still outdoors! Still praise your dog, although not quite as enthusiastically as if he were in the designated area.

Correction

You're also probably wondering what to do if (when) you catch your dog in the act of having an accident indoors!

I cannot stress to you enough how important it is to **NEVER**

CORRECT YOUR DOG UNLESS YOU CATCH HIM IN THE ACT! Three seconds later is too late!

Assuming you do catch your dog in the act, as soon as you see him, exclaim "No!" in a firm, but not yelling voice. As you approach your dog, keep saying "No, no, no, no, no!" Take him by the collar, and guide him to the door and then out to the designated area. Once there, calmly state "Outside, do your business, good boy," (not enthusiastically).

Chances are, your dog is not going to finish making outside after you catch him and interrupt his accident indoors. Your phrase of "outside, do your business, good boy," is intended simply to help make the connection that whenever he does this outside, you're always saying "good boy" and whenever he does this inside, you're correcting "no".

If you are blessed with the rare, but wonderful occasion that your dog *does* finish outside, you'll really need to put on your acting shoes and praise like crazy! This can be a big breakthrough for your dog, and in the interest of teaching him, you'll need to move past your annoyance about the accident and really, really praise lavishly for eliminating outside.

Timing Review

While I realize I'm at risk of sounding repetitive, I feel an additional review of timing is necessary.

Timing is extremely important when praising or correcting your dog. Dogs are very intelligent animals, but they have pretty short attention spans, and take things very literally.

For example, if you praise your dog while the urine is exiting his body, he clearly knows you're praising him for doing his business. But if your dog finished urinating 10 seconds ago and is now looking at a squirrel, he thinks you're praising him for looking at a squirrel!

Likewise, if you correct your dog while he is physically pooping in the guest room, he knows exactly what he's in trouble for. But if you come into the guest room next Thursday and find a petrified poop, and then go get your dog from sleeping on his bed, yelling and dragging him all the way, he will think you're correcting him for sleeping on his bed. Inappropriate timing can be extremely detrimental in house training your dog, harmful to your pet's overall confidence level, and bad for his relationship with you in general. It's of paramount importance to do it right.

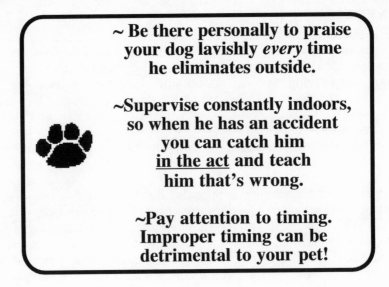

~ Be there personally to praise
your dog lavishly *every* time
he eliminates outside.

~Supervise constantly indoors,
so when he has an accident
you can catch him
<u>in the act</u> and teach
him that's wrong.

~Pay attention to timing.
Improper timing can be
detrimental to your pet!

What to Do if Your Dog Had an Accident & You Didn't Catch Him In The Act

The Proverbial Rolled Up Newspaper

Remember the rolled up newspaper? Used by our grandparents and those before them, this was the accepted method of correcting one's dog for any infraction. Perhaps you yourself have used a rolled up newspaper, either to whack the dog, or to whack your hand, making a corrective noise.

Here is my recommendation for the rolled up newspaper. Take a newspaper, roll it up, and tape it with duct tape so it stays rolled.

When you walk into your dining room and find that your dog pooped there an hour ago, get out the rolled up newspaper.

Now, firmly whack yourself over the head with it! You were supposed to be supervising the dog!

Next, put it in your fireplace and use it for kindling.

The Drag & Show

Another previously common method was to drag your dog over to the accident and "shove his nose in it," followed by putting him out the back door as punishment.

Again, not recommended. Dragging and showing your dog the mess, or any other method of correction administered after the fact will only result in *much more difficulty* teaching your dog. You can end up with a pet who withholds in your presence and is afraid to eliminate in front of you at all. Confusion and fear can also result from after the fact correction, leading to a multitude of additional behavior problems. This will be covered in great detail later in this book in the section, Preventing and Solving Problems.

So What *Should* I Do?

Truthfully, this was a lost opportunity. Every time your dog has an accident and you didn't catch him in the act, you can add approximately three additional days to your housebreaking process. If it only happens once, no big deal...you'll still get great results...no need to admonish yourself too harshly (or to whack yourself with a rolled up newspaper).

However, if your dog is having accidents on a daily, twice weekly, or weekly basis wherein you're not catching him in the act, you'll need to take a close look at your own lack of diligence in supervising. Clearly, you're giving too much unsupervised free time, and you're only making it harder on yourself and your dog by doing so.

If this has been the case, do not despair. As with all things in life, there is still time to make a change. You can begin today, right now, this minute, to more vigilantly supervise your dog. Just because there was a setback does not mean you should give up, or deem your dog untrainable. Make the decision to get on track, and use this as a learning experience.

Be sure to mark down on your Housebreaking Chart (included with this book) the location, approximate time, and "not caught in the act." It really will help pinpoint the times and locations where your dog needs extra walking or supervision.

Meanwhile, do not yell at your dog. Simply clean up the accident using your odor neutralizer, rug cleaner, and paper towels, and move on with your day.

Clean Up

If you thought you were going to house train your dog without having any associated clean up, you were sadly mistaken.

Unfortunately, in order for your dog to learn that eliminating indoors is wrong, you'll need to catch him in the act a few times and correct him. If the methods are followed with extreme diligence, it's possible that some dogs may only require two or three caught and corrected accidents. Some will need a little more reinforcement. Stay with it and it will soon be over.

Neutralize Odors

One of the most important things you can do for clean up is to completely neutralize the odor where the accident occurred. As mentioned in the checklist earlier in this book, I strongly recommend a product called Nature's Miracle. It has special enzymes designed to neutralize odors so they are virtually undetectable to your dog.

Remember that your dog's sense of smell is much more powerful than a human's. You could clean up an accident and not be able to smell it yourself, but your dog probably can. This is why the odor neutralizer is necessary.

For Accidents On Hard Floors

If your dog has an accident on a hard floor such as tile, wood, or linoleum, you're in the best possible shape. Simply wipe it up with a paper towel. Then clean it with whatever product you like (bleach, wood floor cleaner, whatever). Dry thoroughly with more paper toweling. Then use the Nature's Miracle liquid, wipe thoroughly over the area of the accident, and dry with more fresh paper towels.

For Accidents On Rugs or Furniture

These accidents can be more difficult to clean. Hopefully, you've followed the guidelines in the feeding section, and your dog eats only dry food, resulting in firmer, more easily picked up stools.

For liquid accidents, if they've been caught immediately (as they always should be), Nature's Miracle also makes a great product of flakes. Follow the directions on the canister by sprinkling some directly on the accident and leaving it for the prescribed number of minutes to soak up the liquid like a sponge.

After waiting the recommended period of time and removing the flakes, follow with a soaking of Nature's Miracle liquid. (If you didn't catch the accident, and need to clean up later when it's already soaked in, follow the directions starting from the Nature's Miracle soaking part.) Blot and soak up the liquid with paper towels, until you can't get any more liquid out of the carpet or furniture.

To avoid staining, I've also had good results following up with Resolve carpet cleaner. Follow the directions on the bottle.

What Not to Use

Obviously, you should not use bleach to clean your colored carpet. Always check the directions on the bottle before using any cleaning product, and follow their advice about doing a spot test.

Be sure to keep all cleaning products out of the reach of dogs and kids.

But you may be surprised to find out that another thing not to use is ammonia. Because urine also has ammonia-like characteristics, the use of ammonia for cleaning housebreaking accidents can actually serve to *attract* your dog back to that area for another accident. Check your favorite cleaning product and make sure it's not ammonia based before using it to clean up house training accidents.

For convenient links directly to the best prices on the suggested products, visit www.FreeDogTrainingInfo.com and click on "pet supplies."

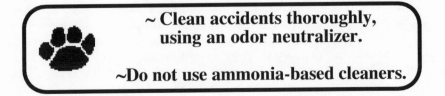

~ Clean accidents thoroughly, using an odor neutralizer.

~Do not use ammonia-based cleaners.

When to Replace
Already Ruined Items

Perhaps your dog has had an ongoing housebreaking problem, and you purchased this book to finally clear up his confusion. Maybe your carpets already have spots and stains all over. It's possible your carpet padding underneath has the odor locked inside, and is beyond thorough cleaning.

This is very common. If it makes you feel any better, you are by far not alone.

Perhaps your dog has had a problem with leg-lifting all over your living room sofa or one particular chair. Your cleaning efforts have not been fruitful, and on damp or humid days, the odor comes wafting out from your favorite easy chair. Also pretty common.

My recommendation, under these circumstances, is to *not* invest in full carpet replacement, or to spend thousands on new living room furniture until after your pet is housebroken.

Temporarily, it can be somewhat helpful to steam clean the carpet and furniture with both a cleaning solution and an odor neutralizer, to diminish the likelihood that your dog will return there for future accidents.

However, some accidents are imminent in house training, and it would not be wise to install beautiful new carpeting until your dog is trustworthy.

If you have only the one particular chair that's been ruined, by all means get rid of it now. Chances are you no longer sit on it anyway. But don't replace it until after your dog's house training is complete.

Here's a tip for a worthwhile investment of your time and/or money. When you are ready to replace the carpet, usually your new carpet will come with free removal of the old when the new one is installed. Very convenient.

The problem is, the carpet guys are very quick...as fast as they have the old carpet and pad removed, the new ones are going in. This means that you will not have time to thoroughly mop and clean the flooring underneath with an odor neutralizer and have time to let it dry before the new carpet goes in. And the men are not going to stand around waiting.

In my experience, it is well worth the additional time and/or money to either: remove the carpet yourself a week before the new installation, giving you plenty of time to clean. Or, pay extra to have them remove the old carpet one day, and install the new one on a different day.

Trust me on this. The last thing you want is for you or your dog to still be able to smell the odors emanating from the flooring two layers deep under your brand new carpet!

Free Time

By now you must be wondering about free time. After all, if you're watching over your dog like a hawk, 24/7, who is actually being trained, him or you?

You're right. Free time has to be given to your pet, but it must be given with lots of forethought and planning. And it must be given gradually, beginning with short periods of time, and starting with small sections of your home at a time.

When is the best time to give free time? When you're positive you have an "empty dog." In other words, you already fed him and gave him water. You personally leash walked him to the bathroom area, saw him both pee and poop, and praised him marching band style. You have just returned indoors and the food and water bowls are no longer available.

Now is the time!

This is the perfect opportunity to play with him in the living room, or let him hang out with you while you clean your child's room. The ideal occasion to let him keep you company while you fold some laundry, pay some bills, or watch T.V.

You'll still need to keep an eye on him though. If you're cleaning your child's room, shut the door so the dog doesn't take off down the hall. If you're vacuuming the house, bring him from room to room with you and shut him into each room as you go along. If you're vacuuming the hall, shut all the room doors so he's only in the hall.

As you progress through the house training process, you'll get to know your dog better. You'll need to gradually start giving him more and more supervised freedom so that in his mind, the den is expanded to include the whole house.

What if you fed and gave water to your dog, and then walked him outside, played with him, gave him some exercise, and an hour later he still hasn't gone to the bathroom? Should you assume that he must not need to go, and choose now as the time to give freedom? No way.

This is the time to supervise him like a hawk, preferably on a hard floor area, and watch for signs to prevent or correct an accident. This is definitely not the time to set him free to go gallivanting through your formal dining room on your imported Persian rug!

Use your best judgment, and when unsure, always err on the side of caution. Remember, your grueling diligence will pay off in a lifetime of enjoying your pet.

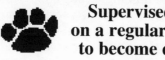 **Supervised free time must be given on a regular basis in order for your pet to become dependably house trained!**

Thorough House Training
Is a 3-Step Process

As with most things, house training your dog is best accomplished by first building a foundation, and then increasing from there. When constructing a house, you don't build the attic before you build the main floor, and you don't build the main floor without building the foundation first. The same is true in dog training.

It is extremely important to make sure you've accomplished the first step before the second, and the second before the third. As we progress through this section, you'll understand why.

The Three Steps of House Training

1) Getting your dog to understand that it is <u>wonderful</u> to eliminate <u>outside</u>.

2) Getting your dog to understand that it is <u>terrible</u> to eliminate <u>inside</u>.

3) Getting your dog to understand that this rule applies to <u>all</u> indoor places, not just his home.

Step 1: Getting Your Dog to Understand That It Is *Wonderful* to Eliminate Outside

In the beginning, your first goal is to <u>prevent</u> any accidents from occurring. This is most easily accomplished by walking, walking, walking. When in doubt, walk your dog to the designated area. During the first week or two, you can't walk your dog too much.

You want to have dozens and dozens of opportunities to praise, praise, praise your dog for "going" outside. "Good boy, do your business, good boy!" A zillion times a day.

If there is even the slightest inkling that your dog might need to go, take him out.

Always use the same door, and follow the same path directly to the designated area. Act like you're there for a purpose, and be sure to praise lavishly when he eliminates.

Your goal for this first step is to get your dog so geared for outside, that he practically drags you directly to the spot, and then grins at you while making.

Your dog should clearly know that it is GREAT to make outside. He should be expecting your praise before you even give it.

Outside is wonderful, wonderful, wonderful!

Step 1 should take anywhere from three days to 10 maximum. If it takes longer, you've likely not been following the feeding, watering, walking, and supervision diligently enough! Only after you've accomplished this goal will you move on to Step 2.

Step 2: Getting Your Dog to Understand That It Is *Terrible* to Eliminate Indoors

Does your dog already drag you directly to the designated area and then grin at you while making? If not, go back to Step 1. If yes, continue on.

Your next task is to get your dog to *gradually* require less number of walks per day, and to learn that when he's indoors he needs to "hold it in" until you walk him. Ideally, you want him to start to tell you when he needs to go out, (there will be another whole section on Teaching Your Dog to Signal When He Needs to Go Out.)

Because you're going to be constantly supervising your dog whenever he's free indoors, you'll have ample opportunity to correct him for having an accident. In fact, you may find that your dog will simply grin right at you and begin to urinate right on the living room floor! Why will he grin? Because so far, you've been praising him every time he goes...outside! He thinks making is good!

Believe it or not, this is good news. Because as soon as you see your dog get ready to have an accident indoors, you will catch him in the act and correct him, "No, no, no, no, no!" all the way to the door, and then bring him to the bathroom area.

There should be a very stark contrast between the lavish praise you've been giving outside, and the firm correction you'll be giving inside. There should be no gray area. It's either wonderful or terrible.

Be careful not to correct your dog so firmly as to scare the wits out of him. Remember, you're *teaching* him, not scaring him!

When you catch your dog in the act of eliminating indoors, the grin will immediately disappear right from his face! At first, he may be confused. He may think to himself, "Hey, usually she always says this is good to do!" This is why it's so important to immediately bring your dog straight out to the designated area and follow with mild praise. You want to reinforce the lesson that whenever he does this inside, you're correcting "no", and whenever he does it outside, you're praising "good boy".

Although you may be tempted, you'll need to scrub the rug *after* you return indoors. You don't want to lose this teaching opportunity by first cleaning and then walking the dog. Timing is everything.

Speaking of timing...when should you correct your dog? If you see him walking around sniffing, should you immediately correct him? What if he's circling around and you're positive he's going to poop...do you wait until he's physically pooping, or correct him as soon as you're certain he's thinking of it?

You're going to have to use your best judgment on this. If your pet is simply walking around sniffing, he might be thinking about peeing, or he might be just sniffing because that's what dogs do. Only correct him if you're positive he's physically beginning to make. On the other hand, if your dog is circling around, and instead of laying down, he gets into the "pooping position," by all means correct him then...no need to wait until it's out. In fact, with perfect timing, you might even be able to correct him and then get him to poop outside. This would be a golden teaching opportunity!

Pretty soon, your dog's attempted accidents will become less and less frequent. You'll be practically home free. In fact, after only three weeks or so, and certainly after your full initial 30 days of vigilant training, he may go months and months without having any accidents! This is great! Until...you bring him to your Mom's house. Read on...

Step 3: Getting Your Dog to Understand That This Applies to *All* Indoor Places, Not Just His Home

I'm sorry to say, I have never come across a dog who was completely house trained for all indoor places without first having (and getting corrected for) an accident in someone else's home.

Remember when we talked about a dog's natural instincts not to soil where they live? Well, if you take your dog to a friend's house, he doesn't feel like he lives there! In his mind, it will be "other than his home" and therefore fair territory for going to the bathroom.

This can best be avoided by making sure your dog eliminates before entering the friend's home. Walk him to an acceptable bush, use his trigger phrase, and make sure you enter the person's house with an empty dog.

But don't get a false sense of security! Knowing what I just explained, you'll need to supervise your dog while visiting, just as diligently as you did in the first days of house training.

If you catch your dog *in the act* of having an accident indoors at someone else's home, it will only take one or two times, and one or two places, before he will permanently understand that the rules apply to all indoor places, not just his home.

What if you just never take him anywhere? You'd be doing yourself and your dog an injustice. Bite the bullet. Get it over with. And for all of his days, you'll have a thoroughly trustworthy pet.

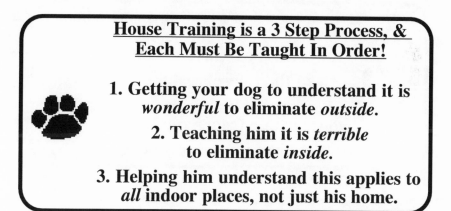

House Training is a 3 Step Process, & Each Must Be Taught In Order!

1. Getting your dog to understand it is *wonderful* to eliminate *outside*.

2. Teaching him it is *terrible* to eliminate *inside*.

3. Helping him understand this applies to *all* indoor places, not just his home.

Housebreaking Guidelines Summary

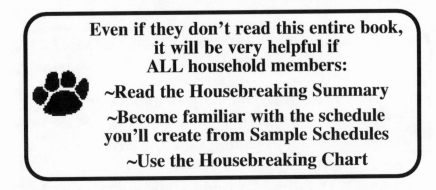

Even if they don't read this entire book, it will be very helpful if ALL household members:

~Read the Housebreaking Summary

~Become familiar with the schedule you'll create from Sample Schedules

~Use the Housebreaking Chart

In order for your dog or puppy to become house trained, it is very important that you strictly follow these guidelines. At first, you may feel sorry for your dog because he will not be allowed free reign of the house very often. It will also be a lot of work for you in the beginning. However, if you stick with it, you will be able to get house training over with quickly, and for the rest of his years, you will have a trustworthy dog.

General Rules

1. Do not let your pet out of the crate at walking times until you are <u>ready to go</u>. If you let your dog out while you prepare coffee, get dressed, or put shoes on, this is ample time for an accident to occur.

2. Do not do other things while your dog waits to go to the bathroom. You must get your pet out as quickly as possible, especially first thing in the morning, or when you've just returned home.

3. Although you may have a fenced yard, it is necessary to *personally leash walk* your dog to the bathroom area <u>every time</u>. You cannot sometimes go with him and other times send him out alone. This seems like a lot of work, but again, if you put in the effort now and get it over with, you will end up with a dog that is house trained, trustworthy, and your yard will stay cleaner and nicer.

4. When we refer to keeping your dog in the crate, we mean with the <u>door closed</u>. If you leave the door open, it is the same as not using the crate at all.

5. Meals will be given to your dog for <u>20 minutes</u>. This is ample time to eat, and it allows you to track your pet's bathroom schedule.
     If you leave food out all day, it will be very difficult to house train your dog. Your dog should remain in the crate (or be personally supervised, eyeball-to-dog-contact) for between 15 minutes and 1 hour and 15 minutes after eating, in order to digest. After that, you'll walk him.

6. Keep track of your dog's <u>water intake</u>. Remember, if you play with him and then give him a bowl of water, you must watch him very closely, or put him in the crate for a while and then walk him again after it's digested (about 5 - 20 minutes).

7. You will get to know your pet's body schedule. If it is a time of day when he usually "does both" (perhaps the after meal walk?), then <u>make sure all business is done</u>. If your dog urinates but does not defecate, he is to go back in the crate (or be personally supervised, eyeball-to-dog-contact) for another 15 - 30 minutes at which time you will try again .

Definitions

<u>Walk-</u> This means that you'll personally leash walk your pet to the outside bathroom area. Encourage your dog to do all business that might be needed. Praise lavishly for eliminating outside.

<u>Food-</u> Your dog should be fed in the crate or kitchen and should stay in the crate to digest, (or be personally supervised, eyeball-to-dog-contact). Food is to be given for 20 minutes.

<u>Water-</u> Your dog can be given water with meals, after play, or any time when you are available to walk him shortly after. Water should not be left out all day, nor left in the crate overnight or when you're out. You

don't want to limit or reduce your dog's water intake. The idea is to keep track of *when* he drank it rather than leaving it out all the time.

Free Time- Free time should be given at times when you've just seen your dog complete all business. Do not give free reign of the whole house all at once. You must keep your dog in a one or two room area, and he must be supervised *every second*.

Crate- These are the times when your dog must stay in the crate...after meals and after bowls of water (to digest until walk), after free time is up, whenever you are out or sleeping, and whenever you cannot supervise (e.g., going in the shower).

      Do not use the crate as a constant crutch though. Free time is very important, but must be accompanied by your personal supervision.

Attention- Don't forget that your pet is a pet. So pet him! Playing, brushing, and petting are great ways to bond with your dog and give each other some love.

Exercise- All dogs need exercise every day. A good run, some ball playing, or other activity is necessary for every dog on a regular basis. If you don't have a fenced yard, use your dog's long line or simply go for a nice long walk together around your neighborhood. Exercise also helps keep digestive processes flowing more regularly.

Obedience- Obedience training is a key ingredient in housebreaking, and in having a good relationship with your dog in general. Basic commands such as "heel," "sit," "down," "stay," "come," and basic manners, should be practiced daily.

Play- An important part of interacting with your pet. Whether you go outside and toss a ball or stay inside and squeak a dog toy, play time is fun for both you and your dog!

Situations

Trigger Phrase- You must choose one phrase that means "pee" and "poop" and <u>use it every time</u>. Choose a command that you and your family will feel comfortable using. Perhaps "do your business," or "go make" might be good choices.

Praise- Be sure to praise your dog lavishly whenever he "goes" outside. <u>Never</u> correct your dog for eliminating outside, even if it is not in the designated area. Praise should include the trigger phrase you are using, (for example, "Good boy, do your business, good boy!")

Correction- In order to correct your dog for having an accident in the house, you must catch your dog in the act.

You must _never, never_ correct your dog unless it is at the moment when he is "going". Correcting him three seconds later is too late. This is why it is so important that you supervise your dog constantly when he is loose in the house.

If you do catch your dog in the act, then you should correct him in a serious manner. "No, no, no, no, no..." as you bring him to the door. Then escort him to the bathroom area. When you get there, you can then reinforce, "Do your business, good boy." Be sure to clean the accident with an odor neutralizer after returning inside.

Your Personal Schedule

Everyone has their own household schedule. Some people live alone. Others live with a roommate, spouse, sibling, or parent. Some people have young children. Some work from home, others work at an outside location. Some are full time, some are part time. Some people are retired, or are full time at-home parents. Some people are temporarily home but will soon be out of the house full time, such as teachers who are off during the summer.

There are a few factors that remain constant no matter what your schedule is. For example, what is the first thing you probably do when you wake up in the morning? Go to the bathroom. Chances are that you don't first read the newspaper, take a shower, or do other things before you attend to your bathroom needs. Likewise, you cannot expect your dog to wait through all that either. Following is a list of several times that your dog must be walked no matter what your particular household is like.

Immediately upon waking up in the morning.
Just before you leave the house for any period of time.
Immediately before going in the crate.
Promptly upon removing from the crate.
Immediately upon your return home.
Before entering the vet, groomer, or someone's home.
Last time out before bed.
Any time you're pretty sure he needs to go.

These are non-negotiable and apply for your dog's lifetime.

Helpful Tips to Make Your Life Easier

~Keep all of the following right by the door through which your dog will be walked:

~Your dog's leash
~A pair of shoes that are easy to slip on and off
~Your jacket
~The Housebreaking Chart and a pencil
~A towel for wiping your dog's paws

~Actually use the Housebreaking Chart: It may seem silly at first, but experience shows that after a few days, you'll begin to see patterns. Analyzing your chart will help you figure out approximately how much time your dog needs to digest food and to digest water. It will also reveal common times that accidents are occurring, common locations of accidents, and may identify a certain time of day when your dog needs an additional walk or better supervision.

Even after over 10 years of being a professional dog trainer, I myself use this chart every single time I am house training a dog. So do many other dog trainers I know.

~Enlist the help of all family members: Do you have a spouse or children? Even children as young as six can walk a dog to the back yard to do his business (unless it's a very large dog). Certainly teenaged kids should not get to just sit around and relax while you do all the work.

Set up a family schedule during which each family member has certain times of day when they handle the walking, and certain times when they're doing the supervising and playing with the dog. It's a great way to teach kids some responsibility, and to take some of the load off the main dog training family member...you! Make sure each person knows exactly what they're supposed to be doing.

To make sure everyone is on the same page, have all family members either read this entire book, or at least the Housebreaking Guidelines Summary (page 54). Everyone should also be made aware of the schedule to be followed (which you'll be creating next), and should utilize the Housebreaking Chart (page 64).

Sample Schedules

As you've studied your way through this book so far, you're probably catching on to what type of schedule you should be following with your dog.

This next section will assist you in creating a personalized plan for house training your dog, which will work with your specific schedule and lifestyle. You'll need to get out a pencil and paper, and prepare your own guidelines that work within your family, work, or school schedule.

No exact schedule can be "carved in stone." Obviously, if you're home and you have the time to personally supervise your dog, you can adjust the schedule accordingly. If he seems like he needs an additional walk, by all means do so. There may be other times when you were planning on your dog having free time, but something's come up so it's got to be changed to a confinement time, and so on.

The basic idea is to monitor your dog's food and water intake, personally leash walk to the bathroom, and confine to the crate when not able to 100% supervise.

That said, I've received an overwhelming amount of requests that I devise sample schedules. Following are some samples I've created. Choose one that best suits your lifestyle, and then adjust accordingly.

Introduction to Sample Schedule #1: For Those Who Work Outside the Home

Remember, no schedule is going to be perfect for everyone. Perhaps you work the night shift, or maybe you work a part time job. The following schedule has been devised assuming you work a traditional 9-5 work day. Feel free to adjust it accordingly.

Keep in mind that when you work full time, your pet may be spending a significant amount of time in the crate. Between work time confinement and sleeping time confinement, it can add up to a lot of time alone.

Therefore, *I highly recommend* stopping home at lunch, hiring a dog walker or local teenager, or making some other midday arrangements for your dog. If there is genuinely no way you can work that out, the absolute maximum any dog should be crated should not ever exceed 8 1/2 hours.

Also, you'll need to spend some time each morning exercising and playing with your pet, and plenty of time in the evening too.

Gone are the days of stopping off to do errands on the way home, going for drinks with coworkers, or any other activity that will result in your dog being home alone more than the maximum amount of time. This holds true not only for the house training period, but for your dog's lifetime.

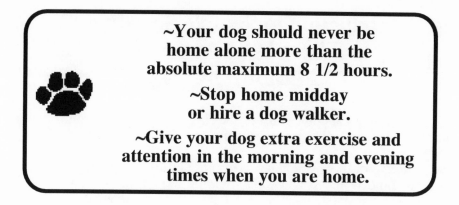

~Your dog should never be home alone more than the absolute maximum 8 1/2 hours.

~Stop home midday or hire a dog walker.

~Give your dog extra exercise and attention in the morning and evening times when you are home.

Sample Schedule For Those Who Work Outside the Home

6:30 am- Walk and attention.
6:45 am- Food and water.
7:15 am- Walk and attention.
7:45 am- Supervise (or crate if absolutely necessary).
8:15 am- Walk, exercise, obedience, play, and finish with final walk before work.
8:45 am- Crate.
12:15 pm- Walk, water, attention, and exercise. Finish with walk before returning to work.
12:45 pm- Crate.
5:15 pm- Walk and attention.
5:30 pm- Food and water.
6:00 pm- Walk and attention.
6:30 pm- Supervise (or crate if absolutely necessary).
7:30 pm- Walk, exercise, obedience, and play. Supervised free time...bring in other rooms. Add additional walk as necessary if you feel needed during this time.
9:30 pm- Last water of the day. Supervise.
10:15 pm- Last walk, some exercise and attention. Finish with walk before bed.
10:30 pm- Crate overnight.

Don't forget to use the Housebreaking Chart, included at the end of this chapter!

Introduction to Sample Schedule #2: For Those Who Are At Home Most of The Day

If you are at home most of the day, you may think you'll have a much easier time house training your dog. That may be true, or it may not.

Remember, your dog needs to build up muscle control so he can learn to "hold it in." If you walk your dog too much, or allow constant access to outside (such as using a doggy door, keeping your door propped open, or having him live mostly outside), he will not develop that control.

Even if you're at home, you'll still need to confine your dog for periods of time. This will help him develop his muscles, prepare for days when you will be out, and also prevent other behavior problems, such as separation anxiety.

Keep in mind, I don't know exactly what schedule would perfectly suit you. Some people are early to bed, early to rise. Others like to sleep in or may be more of a night owl. Therefore, I've created the following schedule keeping in mind that many at home people are either parents (who are typically up somewhat early), or perhaps retired and may be in the early-rise habit after years of working. Of course, feel free to adjust the schedule so it suits you best.

Even if you are at home most of the day, you'll still need to confine your dog on a regular basis. This will build up your pet's muscle control, a mandatory part of being house trained.

Sample Schedule
For Those Who Are At Home
Most of The Day

7:00 am- Walk and attention.
7:30 am- Food & water.
8:00 am- Walk and attention.
8:30 am- Crate.
11:00 am- Walk, exercise, obedience, and play. Supervised free time...bring in other rooms. Add additional walk as necessary, if you feel needed during this time.
12:00 pm- Water.
12:15 pm- Walk.
12:30 pm- Crate.
3:30 pm- Walk, exercise, obedience, and play. Supervised free time...bring in other rooms. Add additional walk as necessary, if you feel needed during this time.
5:30 pm- Food & water.
6:00 pm- Walk.
6:30 pm- Crate.
8:30 pm- Walk, exercise, obedience, and play. Supervised free time...bring in other rooms. Add additional walk as necessary, if you feel needed during this time.
9:30 pm- Last water of the day. Supervise.
10:15 pm- Last walk, some exercise and attention. Finish with walk before bed.
10:30 pm- Crate overnight.

Don't forget to use the Housebreaking Chart, next page!

HOUSEBREAKING CHART

This chart has been designed to help you keep track of your dog's bathroom habits. You'll be recording feeding and watering times, walking times, when your dog "did his business," and when/where accidents occurred. For accidents, you'll also keep track of whether or not you caught your pet in the act. Use of this chart will enable you to more accurately predict your dog's needs, and identify certain times when an additional walk or increased supervision is necessary. Remember, your diligence will pay off in years of a trustworthy, housebroken pet!

Once you've filled up this page, simply get out some paper and a ruler, and continue the chart on your own, or create an identical chart on your computer using a spreadsheet program.

Dog's Trigger Phrase:

FEEDING or WATERING TIME (Write 'food' or 'water')	WALKING TIME (Write it every time, even if he didn't 'go')	URINATED OUTSIDE	DEFECATED OUTSIDE	ACCIDENT: LOCATION & TIME.... (Caught in act? Write 'caught' or 'not caught')
Food & Water 7:00 am	7:15 am	√	—	
	7:35 am	—	√	8:45 am Urinated in kitchen - caught

64

Analyzing Your Housebreaking Chart

As your Housebreaking Chart becomes filled in, you'll be able to analyze how things are going and use that information to figure out how best to help your dog.

For example, in the sample shown the dog was walked twice after the food and water. The first time he urinated only. The second time he defecated only.

Figuring she had an empty dog, our pretend dog owner must have decided to give free time, because at 8:45 the dog urinated in the kitchen. Fortunately, her pet was caught in the act.

It could be a coincidence that the dog had an accident at that time. But what if the pretend dog owner analyzes the chart after a week and notices her dog had an accident another day around the same time?

Logically, she would assume the dog requires an additional walk at this time of day. If she's not available to walk him at that time, he'll need to stay in the crate until she can walk him shortly thereafter.

Similarly, you'll need to analyze your chart on a regular basis to help identify times when your pet can benefit from additional supervision, an extra walk, or some confinement time.

Diligent use of this chart will help immensely in your effort to train your pet.

Part II

Preventing & Solving Problems

Introduction to Preventing & Solving Problems

Congratulations on completing the first part of this book! At this juncture, you should have a strong understanding of how your dog thinks, and a clear idea of what steps need to be taken for house training.

Even if your dog doesn't seem to be having any particular problems, you can learn a whole bunch from this section. Preventing & Solving Problems will give you lots of insight into common errors to avoid, so your dog's house training can be accomplished as quickly and thoroughly as possible.

If you are having some specific issues with your dog, I've done my best to think of all the usual and not-so-usual problems that sometimes occur. As you read through this section, chances are that all of your questions will be answered. If you take my advice seriously and make the recommended changes, your dog can soon be the housebroken, trustworthy pet you've always wanted.

Let's continue!

My Dog is Having Accidents In the Crate!

     This is a problem that sometimes occurs with very young puppies who simply can't hold it, or older dogs who have never built up muscle control before.

     Any dog purchased in a pet store is also significantly more likely to have this issue in the beginning. However, if you diligently stick with the methods in this book, your dog will come around!

     Remember, dogs instinctively don't like to soil where they live. Therefore, our first goal is to get the dog or puppy to keep his crate clean. Certainly, if he doesn't mind soiling in the crate, he will not mind soiling in the living room!

     Begin by always feeding your pet his meals inside the crate. This will help define the crate as a "food area," and will help bring out your dog's natural inclination to keep it clean.

     Also, make sure your dog's crate is small enough that he doesn't have enough room to eliminate in one corner and then go rest in another corner. The crate should be just large enough for your dog to stand, sit, and lie down. It should not be large enough to walk around, do jumping jacks, or rest away from the mess.

     If you need to make your dog's crate temporarily smaller, and don't want to buy a smaller crate, you have several options: purchase a special panel made for this purpose, build a divider panel out of plywood and secure it with strong ties, or use plastic milk crates to fill up the back half of the crate. Do not use cardboard. If you build your own barrier, take all safety measures into consideration: make sure your dog cannot get his paws stuck, and do not use any material he could chew or eat.

     There is also the occasional intelligent male dog who has figured out that he can lift his leg and get the urine to land *outside* the crate. If you're having this problem, you'll need to build "splash backs" for the outside of the crate. They should go halfway up, on all four sides of the crate. They can be made inexpensively and easily by first measuring, and then visiting your local home center. They will cut the sturdy, clear Plexiglas pieces for you, you'll need to drill some holes, and they can then be attached with wire strong ties. See diagram on page 71.

     If your dog has been having accidents of any kind in the crate, you'll also need to remove any and all bedding, blankets, or any other fabric from the crate. This is because if your dog urinates on a towel, the towel will soak up the urine and it will mostly stay in that one spot. Your dog can then stay in the other part of the crate and it won't seem so dirty.

If there is no towel, then when your dog urinates, it will run down along the whole tray, therefore making your dog feel more like he's stuck with it. Initially, this may make things worse for you, because your dog may get a bit dirtier at first. However, after only a few experiences like this, your pet will be much more inclined to work on his bladder control.

Make sure you're also doing obedience training with your dog on a daily basis. This can help immensely. For a review, re-read the Obedience chapter (page 37). Don't underestimate the value of practicing the commands...it can really make a significant difference almost immediately.

If you've tried the above methods for a full 10 days, and your dog is over 14 weeks old, you'll need to examine your own methods and schedule to figure out the problem. Either you're not walking him often enough, or you're not following his digestion schedule closely enough, or perhaps you're simply out too long of a time.

I've occasionally come across a client whose dog is having a problem due to a urinary tract infection. Such an infection would also be accompanied by other symptoms, such as extremely frequent urinating even when you are home. Most of the time accidents in the crate are behavioral, but if you feel your dog is having these symptoms, a vet visit would be a good idea.

In some cases, if your dog absolutely, 100% of the time, _never has accidents in the house or crate when you're home_, the problem at hand might be separation anxiety rather than a housebreaking problem.

If this is so, you may need to work with a professional trainer to fully resolve the separation anxiety problem. Also, visit www.FreeDogTrainingInfo.com for free articles and tips on separation anxiety, and what you can do to help your pet on your own.

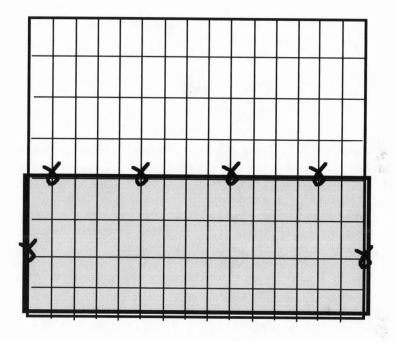

*For male dogs who lift their leg to make the urine go
outside the crate, you can create "splash backs".*

*Use sturdy, clear Plexiglas around the lower half of the crate on
all four sides. Attach to the outside, using wire strong ties.*

My Dog Doesn't Seem to Realize What He's Supposed to Do In the Designated Area!
(Or He's Partial To a Different Spot)

Some dogs may be in the habit of using a different spot for their outdoor eliminating. Perhaps in the past, your dog was in the habit of urinating right outside the back door. Or maybe you used to leave him loose and he preferred pooping in front of the shed, rather than in the corner you've selected.

Sometimes puppies are so silly and distracted when they're outdoors, they don't seem to be picking up on the fact that they're supposed to be going to the bathroom!

The first thing to do is review your selection of the designated bathroom area. Does it afford your dog some privacy? Is the spot too close to a major distraction zone (such as a corner where your yard meets another yard with a barking dog)? Is it close enough to the house to be realistic, yet far enough that it's acceptable to you too?

If your review reinforces your belief that you've chosen an appropriate spot, continue to the next step. Otherwise, consider a different area that meets those important criteria.

There is an excellent product on the market called Puppy Housebreaking Aide. Fondly referred to by us dog trainers as "disgusting stuff". Basically, this is a product that mimics the smell of dog urine, with the intention of triggering the dog's instinct to eliminate in spots where other dogs have gone. It is available as a spray, a dropper applicator, or as a post in the ground. All work, but I prefer the drops.

Warning! This stuff truly smells very strongly of urine! You only need the *tiniest, tiniest* amount to scent the area. If you use the spray, make sure you or your dog are not standing down wind so it doesn't get on you.

Remember, dogs have a much stronger sense of smell than humans. You only need one or two tiny drops in the corner of the designated area, to achieve the goal of bringing out your dog's instinct to eliminate there. In fact, if you use too much, your dog may not want to go there at all because it will not seem clean.

A little exercise can help burn off the sillies for a dog who is extremely distracted or excited. Practicing the obedience commands for a few minutes can also help get your pet's attention focused on you and the business at hand.

Often, scenting the area as described above can help your dog to realize why you keep hanging around in this spot. Combined with following a feeding and watering schedule, diligence in personally leash walking to the area, some exercise and obedience, your dog will soon give you the opportunity to praise him for eliminating in the desired section.

Please remember that although your goal is for your pet to use the designated area, you must *never* correct him for making in a different spot outdoors. It is still outside! Simply praise lightly and increase your diligence by keeping him with you in the designated area until after he's done his business, before giving free time in the yard.

For convenience in purchasing Puppy Housebreaking Aide, visit our easy click-on lists in the "pet supplies" section at www.FreeDog TrainingInfo.com.

My Dog Only Has Accidents In a Certain Spot!

There are a couple of reasons why a dog will repeatedly have accidents in a specific spot or two.

The first is that dogs are creatures of habit. If there was a spot where he's habitually had accidents in the past, he's much more likely to return to that area.

Another scenario is when the dog is seemingly housebroken, but occasionally will go and have an accident in a place such as a formal dining room, guest room, or basement. In this case, it's usually because those are areas where your dog doesn't normally spend much time. Therefore in his mind, it's "other than where he lives," and fair game for eliminating. For a review, see Expanding the Den (page 5).

The best way to resolve this problem is to first thoroughly clean the area with an odor neutralizer, as discussed in the chapter on Clean

Up (page 45).

Next, begin spending more time with your dog in that room, and specifically around that spot. You want your dog to think of this as a "clean section," part of his home where *he lives*, and therefore doesn't want to soil.

For example, if your dog occasionally has accidents in your formal dining room, you'll need to start practicing obedience in there, sit on the floor with him, pet and brush him in that room, and even feed him his meals, with his dish on the very spot where the accidents used to occur.

While it is not thrilling to have your dog spend more time in your formal dining room (the very beast you didn't want in there in the first place!), it is better to do this now than to occasionally find a land mine cohabitating with your special dining room furnishings!

 Remember, your dog must feel like *he* lives in all the parts of your home!

My Dog Occasionally Urinates on My Bed!

There are some people whose dogs have chosen to have their occasional "accidents" right on the owner's bed, pillows, or other belongings. In these instances, they aren't actually accidents at all!

If your dog is choosing areas that clearly have your scent, it is a sure sign that your pet is trying to dominate you. Usually, the dog will choose an area that is clearly the owner's "den," such as the bed or couch.

This is most common with male dogs who have not been neutered, or with male or female dogs around 1 1/2 years of age (although it could happen with any age or gender). Intact male dogs have a much stronger instinct to mark their territory. Dogs who are around 1 1/2 years of age are coming into their adult maturity and may be testing the boundaries to see if they can rise within the pecking order.

The first solution is to immediately stop reading this book, and go phone your vet for an appointment to have your dog neutered. It is not going to make your dog be "less of a man," or an ineffective watch dog. In fact, neutering can contribute to good behavior, a better relationship with your pet, and can reduce the risks of numerous health problems. For more info on this, please re-read the chapter on Spaying and Neutering (page 35).

However, neutering alone will not solve this problem. If your dog truly respected you as the leader of the pack, he would not even consider putting his scent on your territory! You will need to work on more consistent obedience training, and start making your dog "earn his keep" within your household. In other words, start exerting your leadership in many little ways during day-to-day life.

For example, when your dog barks at you while you're on the phone, do not keep throwing his toy to keep him quiet. If you do, that means *he* has trained *you* to throw the toy whenever he demands!

Instead, next time your dog barks while you're on the phone, ask your friend to hold the line a moment, and put your dog in a down/stay. In this way *you'll* be training *him* that when you're on the phone, he's to lay quietly.

This is not to say that you shouldn't play with your dog and throw his toy...it's just that it should be on your terms. For a refresher, please refer to the chapters Understanding How Dogs Think (page 4), and Obedience Makes a Huge Difference (page 37).

Other ideas for earning his respect include making sure he sits and stays for food, water, or treats, not allowing him to pull you when you go for a walk, and most of all, being consistent...always proving to your pet that *you* are more stubborn than him in every situation.

If you've been slacking off in the obedience practicing department, now is the time to pick up again. Work your dog through the obedience commands for at least 10 minutes, three times per day. Use the commands as a part of life on a daily basis. Teach your dog something new, and earn his respect by following through and being consistent. You can do it, and it will work!

I Walk My Dog For an Hour, He Won't Go, & Then Has an Accident as Soon as We Return Indoors!

For Puppies Only

If you have a puppy, it may be as simple as your dog being distracted when you're outside. If your puppy is staring at squirrels, eating sticks, or otherwise not paying attention, you'll need to help him focus on the business at hand.

Be sure to walk your dog only to the designated area. In other words, don't cover lots of territory if your mission is to go to the bathroom. Remember, each inch of new territory contains lots of new sensory distractions for puppies to discover. Keep your dog focused on bathroom duties by staying in the designated bathroom area.

Your dog may also be in need of some exercise and stimulation. If you've tried the designated area and he's just way too distracted, you can also try walking him around a bit, letting him sniff, playing some ball, or letting him get a good run out of his system (assuming he's fully vaccinated). Then, return to the designated area for bathroom purposes before heading indoors.

Let's say you've done all of the above, and your dog still hasn't eliminated. Should you just assume he doesn't need to go, and set him free to roam about the house unsupervised? Definitely not. If your puppy has not gone in hours, or has consumed a meal and/or water, you'll need to return him to his crate and try walking him again in another half hour or so.

On the other hand, if your dog just did his business a few minutes ago and you were only walking him again because he stood near the door, you might let him have *supervised* free time, in a small area of your home. You'll need to use your judgment on this, as you're the one who knows when he last ate, drank, or eliminated.

For Puppies & Older Dogs: Withholding

There are some dogs who will exhibit this behavior due to a much more complicated misunderstanding. Unfortunately, this can be extremely frustrating, but it can be alleviated.

Remember the numerous times during this book when I told you that owners should *never, never* correct their dog for an accident unless he was caught *in the act*? Also, think back to the chapter entitled Housebreaking is a 3 Step Process. Remember, the *first* step is to get your dog to understand that it *is wonderful* to do his business outside.

Herein lies the problem...you just recently started following the methods in this book! Perhaps you've made some mistakes in the past, and maybe you have corrected your dog after the fact. Maybe you didn't make that particular mistake, but perhaps you've not been outdoors to tell him that outside *is* good. In these cases, here's the problem:

Your dog may think *all* urinating and defecating is bad, not necessarily only indoors!

Therefore, he doesn't want to make in front of you at all, even outside! This can be very frustrating for owners who walk and walk their dog, standing outside for hours on end, only to have the dog eliminate inside the minute they blink an eye! It will be difficult, but this can be overcome in a matter of days. Read on!

If you are pretty certain that your dog is withholding because he thinks all eliminating is bad and doesn't want to make in front of you, you'll need to exercise extra diligence in *preventing* accidents indoors. In fact, you'll need to do whatever is necessary to make sure no accidents occur, even if that means walking your dog a zillion times a day and never taking your eyes off of him unless he's in his crate.

If your dog does have an accident, and you haven't already taught him that outside is wonderful, you may even need to *not* correct him, until after you've *first* taught him that outside is good. This applies only to dogs who are having this withholding problem.

Remember, there's only so long he can hold it in! If you walk and walk, supervise and supervise, eventually, he will be so full, he will *have to* make in front of you outside, and you'll get a chance to praise him. Let me share a personal story with you...

Years ago, before I was a dog trainer, I had a dog named Winnie. We lived in a house with a fenced yard and I had a schedule that allowed me to sometimes work from home. I'd let her out numerous times a day, and she'd spend a good 20 minutes at a clip in the yard. I'd figure, since she'd been outdoors for awhile, she must have "gone," because that's what dogs do. Also, when I did go out in the yard, there were plenty of poop piles to be cleaned up, so I knew she definitely was doing some business out there.

I had read that I should never correct my dog unless she was caught in the act. For the first few weeks I never corrected her unless it was at the moment she was going. If I did catch her, I'd yell "No, no, no!" and I'd put her out the back door.

After about a month or so, she would never have accidents in front of me anymore. But just as soon as I'd figure she was housebroken, I'd let her in from the yard, go into the shower, and return 15 minutes later to find an accident on the floor! Exasperated, I'm sorry to admit, I did a few times drag her over, show her the mess, and put her out the back door (remember, I was not yet a dog trainer!)

This went on awhile longer, and soon it was time to attend dog training school, where I lived in the school dormitory and my dog lived in the student kennel for several months.

One thing about dog training school was, there was no fenced yard! The only way for students to address our pets' elimination needs was to retrieve them from the student kennel and personally leash walk our dogs to the designated area.

Well, I personally leash walked my dog. And I walked her. And walked her. I walked her at 6 am, 7 am, and from 8-9 am. Then I went to class. I walked her at 12 noon, and from 12:30-1:00. Then I walked her again at 5 pm, 6 pm, from 7-9 pm, 10 pm, 11 pm, and 12 am!! And you know what? She didn't poop for three days!

That's right, three days! Mind you, this was all taking place in Ohio during late winter/spring. It was freezing cold and pouring rain almost constantly. I was living in shared quarters with 12 other people, and sleeping in a room the size of a walk in closet. My (formerly very spoiled) dog was living in a *kennel*, and on top of it, I was worried that she was going to get sick from not defecating for days on end. It was very traumatic!

In addition, whenever she wasn't personally being leash walked by me outside, she had to stay in the kennel. There was to be no free time until she'd eliminated outside. I had to *first* get her to understand it *is wonderful* to make outside before I could risk her having an accident indoors.

By the way, at least two other students were having the same problem. One girl was so upset, she even slept in the kennel for two nights because she was so worried her dog would be sick!

I promise there is a point to this story. The point is, on the fourth morning, my dog could not hold it in a moment longer. I was walking her and walking her, we were both soaking wet from rain, and it wasn't even completely light out yet. Finally, the poop practically exploded from her body, in spite of her best efforts to keep it in.

She looked at me with complete horror, fully expecting me to yell at her.

I still remember the confused look on her face as I quietly praised her, "Good girl, Winnie. Good girl, do your business!" I continued saying "good girl" quietly until she finished, and then I broke out the marching band! I petted her, tossed the ball, and we roughhoused. I even let her jump on me in a joyous, muddy celebration as I praised her like she did the greatest thing on earth!

This was a big breakthrough. The next time she defecated in front of me only took 1 1/2 days of constant walking. Within a week, she was eliminating like a normal dog, twice a day like clockwork. And you know what else? She was grinning right at me while she did it. She'd learned it *is wonderful* to make outside!

Was this fun to do? Absolutely not. Would I wish this on any of you? Never. But if I can do it, and dozens of clients over the years have ironed this out with their dogs, so can you. It will not be easy. It will not be relaxing. But it can be done, and you have no other choice. Letting your dog have a permanent housebreaking problem is simply not an option.

I can hear all the doubts and explanations going through your mind..."But I have kids to take care of!" "I have work to do!" "I can't devote that much time to this!"

All of these things are true. But in the grand scheme of things, devoting four whole days to making it over this important hurdle will be well worth 15 years of enjoying a housebroken dog. So find a way, and get walking!

If your dog has housebreaking confusion that has led to a withholding problem, you'll need to walk & crate, walk & crate, walk & crate...24/7...and soon you'll get the opportunity to praise your pet for eliminating outside.

My Dog Refuses to Go Outside in the Rain!
(Or cold, hot, wind, etc.)

This is a quite frequent scenario: the human opens the door, the dog sees the rain, and turns right around to head back inside. Or maybe he does initially step outside, but then just stands there, all stiff, as if the rain is hurting him.

The dog stays focused on getting back inside, rather than on the "business" at hand. Then, later he ends up having an accident because he didn't eliminate when he was outside!

Not coincidentally, pets having this problem are frequently owned by humans who also dislike being outside in the rain. Most often, this issue exists in households where the dog is just sent outside to do his business, rather than personally leash walked.

If this situation (or similar) applies to you, remember...you purchased this book planning on preventing or alleviating potty problems with your dog. Also remember, for house training purposes, you'll be personally leash walking your dog every single time, even if it's inclement weather. In fact, for your dog it's *especially* important in bad weather because his history shows that's when he's more likely to have accidents!

Begin by purchasing a good raincoat (for yourself), and an umbrella. Keep them conveniently near the door you normally use when you walk your dog. Of course, you already have a towel by the door for drying your pet when you return indoors, as always.

Next time it's raining, use leadership body language to show your dog that going out in the rain is perfectly normal. Throw on your raincoat, clip on your dog's leash, and walk him to the designated area just like you would on a dry day. If he keeps straining back toward the house, give a gentle tug on the leash, have him heel (walk at your side) with you a little, and then remind him, "Do your business!"

For pets who are extremely nervous about the inclement weather, it may also help to run around with him a bit, toss the ball, practice obedience, or do other things to get him to realize that even in the rain, he can still act normally.

Yes, he may get wetter and dirtier than you'd like. Your hair may get messed up and your shoes may get muddy. But overall it will be worth it...you'll have a house trained dog, even in the rain!

> **Dogs, being pack animals will look to their Alpha for guidance.**
>
> **Use leadership body language to show your dog that it's fine to act normally, even in inclement weather... and he'll follow suit!**

Leg Lifting or Territorial Marking Indoors

If your dog is lifting his leg along your furniture, trash can, or other areas of your home, you have more than just a housebreaking issue. You also have a respect problem.

More common with male dogs, but also sometimes with females, territorial marking can be a serious problem to say the least.

The first step is to make sure your dog is spayed or neutered. This can help considerably in cutting down on the dog's natural instinct to mark his scent all over the place. For a more detailed explanation, please review the chapter entitled Spaying and Neutering (page 35).

The next step is to realize that this is your dog's way of dominating the household! Perhaps he's trying to dominate you (as in "My dog urinates along my easy chair"). Or maybe he's trying to dominate someone else, (for example; the baby's room, the cat's scratching post, your other dog's bed, etc.).

Truthfully, if your dog is dominating the household by marking his scent, house training is only the tip of your problem! Dogs who feel they're in charge are also significantly more likely to "discipline" others with aggressive behavior, be possessive over their food, or at the very least, be much less of a listener in general.

In order to alleviate this problem, you'll need to do <u>all</u> of the following:

1) Make an appointment to get your dog spayed or neutered.

2) While your dog is at the vet getting that done, go around and thoroughly clean all of the affected areas with an odor neutralizer. For more information on cleaning, see the chapter on Clean Up (page 45).

3) When your dog returns from the vet, you'll be advised to have your dog take it easy for a few days. During this time, be sure to confine your dog to an area where he's not likely to urinate. Supervise constantly, preventing the marking from recurring.

4) As soon as your dog has sufficiently healed, get to work on some obedience training. Work with your dog on a leash all around your house, especially in the areas where he's marked in the past.

5) Earn your dog's respect in additional ways too. Some suggestions: do not allow your dog on furniture or beds. Make your dog sit/stay before receiving food, water, a treat, or petting. Discontinue letting your pet train you into doing things...like throwing the ball because he barks at you while you're on the phone. Work on the heel command, so your dog no longer pulls you when you walk him. And make any other necessary changes so he no longer feels like he's in charge of the household.

6) Follow the housebreaking schedule and chart as outlined throughout this book. Personally leash walk your dog outside to do his business and praise lavishly. Regulate feeding and watering schedules, and supervise or confine when indoors.

7) Supervise your pet constantly when indoors. Look for opportunities to catch him *in the act* of marking on things. You don't have to wait until he's physically urinating. If you see him sidling up to the easy chair and are positive his plan is to urinate, go ahead and correct him then. Be particularly diligent in areas that have been a problem in the past. Never correct your dog after the fact. For a more detailed explanation of this extremely important timing issue, re-read the chapter Praise & Correction, beginning on page 40.

Remember, dogs are instinctively pack animals. While you may not be able to change the pecking order between your dog and your newborn, you certainly can change the pecking order between *you* and your dog.

If your dog clearly sees you as the Alpha, he wouldn't dare mark his scent in your territory...your territory being the entire house and all of its contents! Obedience will be paramount in resolving this issue. For a more detailed discussion, see Obedience Makes a Huge Difference (page 37).

Submissive or Excitement Urinating

For Both Submissive & Excitement Wetters

Some dogs have a problem wherein they accidentally tinkle a bit when they either get excited or are feeling submissive. This can be very annoying when visitors arrive and get their shoes sprinkled on, or at the very least, you need to clean the floor.

Both submissive and excitement urinating are not actually house training problems. They are behavioral issues. The dog does not even realize there's anything coming out. But since this is a book about "all things pee and poo," I will guide you through eliminating these issues.

Generally, these problems are more common in puppies and in dogs owned by people who are at home all day. Both of those groups of dogs tend to have less bladder control in general, due to their young age or overly frequent walking.

Therefore, no matter what age or breed of dog, and no matter what type of household schedule you keep, the first step is to follow a strong house training regimen so your dog can build up maximum muscle control. For those of you who are at home, please review the Introduction at the beginning of Sample Schedule #2: For Those Who Are at Home Most of The Day (page 62).

There are some breeds of dogs who are notorious for having these excitement or submissive urinating problems. Among them is the Cocker Spaniel. However, let me assure you that in all the years of working with various breeds of dogs, even Cocker Spaniels (and dogs of every breed) *can* stop having this problem. Stop convincing yourself that your dog can't learn, and he *will* learn.

In addition to following a diligent house training schedule and confining your dog regularly so he builds up muscle control, you'll also need to implement an obedience training program. Whether you work with your dog on your own or with a trainer, you'll need to use obedience to alleviate the problem.

If your dog is a submissive urinator, obedience training will be a confidence builder.

If your dog is an excitement wetter, obedience will help him remain more calm during stimulating situations.

Work with your dog on the basic obedience commands of "heel," "sit," "down," "stay," and "come." Also accomplish basic manners: no jumping, pulling, bolting out the door, play biting, stealing food, etc.

Once your pet has learned the commands, you can use the sit/stay during exciting (or what he perceives as intimidating) situations. Generally, a dog who is fully in a "sit" position, cannot also urinate.

By teaching your dog to be more confident, he's less likely to feel so submissive in the first place. Learning to be more calm will also help excited dogs not to tinkle during the stimulating moments.

Sometimes it can help to encourage your dog to hold a toy in his mouth during exciting times, although this alone will not be the entire solution. For some pets, it can almost serve as a pacifier to help them draw upon their willpower to behave more calmly.

Also keep in mind that dogs communicate through body language and eye contact. When you or others greet your dog, do so by facing him with the side of your body, rather than looming above him with the front of your body, which could intimidate some pets.

Discourage visitors from using very excited voices when greeting your pet, and you do the same. In fact, at first it may be best to ignore your dog for the initial few minutes until he gets the sillies out and starts acting more relaxed.

For Submissive Urinating Only

Occasionally I've come across a client who is convinced that their dog pees on purpose. "He always does it when I yell at him!" is a common exclamation. "He's being spiteful and trying to get back at me for yelling."

While this may seem to be the case, rest assured that as intelligent as dogs are, he is not smart enough to figure out that if he urinates, he'll be "getting you back." In fact, I don't know any dogs who enjoy being yelled at, and if he was that smart he'd also be wise enough to know his sprinkling is only going to make you madder.

Instead, alleviate this problem by working with your pet appropriately. Do not yell at the top of your lungs. Do not loom over him, whack a newspaper, hit him, or do any other intimidating things. Those actions are only likely to further deteriorate your dog's confidence, leading to additional wetting and other problems.

Instead, use neutral body language (face him with the side of your body), implement an obedience training and confidence building/ socialization program, and use a much more appropriate and calm method of correction if your dog does do something wrong.

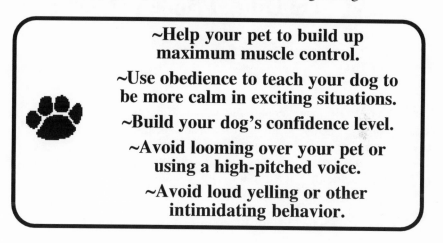

~Help your pet to build up
maximum muscle control.

~Use obedience to teach your dog to
be more calm in exciting situations.

~Build your dog's confidence level.

~Avoid looming over your pet or
using a high-pitched voice.

~Avoid loud yelling or other
intimidating behavior.

When You and Your Dog Move to a Different Home
(Also, Vacationing With Your Pet or Visiting Other People's Homes)

A very common scenario is when someone has a dog who has been thoroughly house trained for several years. Then one day, they move to a new home and their pet starts having accidents!

This is one of the ironies of life. Just when you don't want your dog to have accidents (in your new place), and you also have no extra time for teaching (you have a whole house to unpack), that's exactly when he needs some extra attention and training!

Remember what we talked about in Expanding the Den (page 5)? Housebreaking builds off of your dog's natural instinct not to want to soil in the same place where he *lives*. Well, to your dog, the new place is "other than where he lives" and therefore, potentially okay for eliminating!

I'd like to share a personal story with you. My husband and I are both Certified Master Dog Trainers. We have a Black Labrador named Sam. We also have two cats and two kids. When our dog was about nine years old (and certainly thoroughly house trained with designated area and free run), and our children were three and five years old, we moved from New York to North Carolina.

You can probably imagine how much work this was for us. Between packing everything, selling our old house and business, buying our new house and setting up our business, arranging for movers, driving 13 hours with two small kids and three pets, and having an entire house to unpack and set up, it is safe to say we had no "extra" time to train the dog.

On top of it, our old house had a fenced yard with a designated area and our new yard didn't. We wanted Sam to learn to use a new designated spot, and we knew it was important to follow a house training schedule because it was a new home. So we did. We fed and gave him water at scheduled times. We personally leash walked him to the new designated area. We mostly supervised him when we he was indoors.

86

Things seemed to be going great.

Of course, our first priorities were unpacking our children's things, and the kitchen. We kept an eye on Sam for the most part, figuring he's trustworthy, we've been walking him, and he should be fine.

Until day three, when we walked into the play room (where none of us had spent any time yet,) and there was a big poop! We almost couldn't believe it, except we realized that we hadn't taught him that this room is part of our home! He knew the living room, our bedrooms, kitchen, etc., were part of the "den" because we were all spending time there. But not the play room.

So what did we do? We forced ourselves to *make time* for several sessions every day, familiarizing our pet with that room. We practiced obedience, played ball, brushed him, and even fed him in there a few times.

Within two days he realized this was part of our home. There were no more accidents, he was back to being trustworthy, with free run of the house, and using his designated spot outside.

In addition, we kept walking him to the designated area for several weeks so he would dependably use only that spot and not the whole yard.

Was this fun or relaxing? Absolutely not. But it was worth it because there were no more accidents in our new home and our yard stays clean and nice.

If we can carve out time for this with three pets, two small kids, a new business, and a new home in a new state, I'm certain you can teach your pet when you move too!

Vacationing With Your Pet or Bringing Him to Visit Other's Homes

By the way, the same concept applies to vacationing or visiting other people's homes. You'll need to keep in mind that it's not your dog's normal home, so he may not realize right off the bat that there are to be no accidents.

If you have a dog of any age who has not yet proven himself trustworthy at home, or you have a puppy who might also chew or do other potentially harmful things, be sure to bring his crate...for your own peace of mind and that of your host.

Do the leash walking, food and water monitoring, and supervising or confining, and things will work out just fine.

House Training and
The Rescued Dog

Imagine you lived in a foreign land. You always spoke a certain language, did things a certain way, and followed certain rituals or traditions. Suddenly one day, you arrive in America, and things are different here! You're not sure what customs are acceptable, and which ones are not. Chances are, you would really wish you had a guide to *teach* you the ways of the land.

Although I am not a dog, I imagine this is much how a rescued dog must feel. Perhaps he used to live in the street. Maybe he was previously in a neglectful or abusive home. It's possible he was in a nice home where the people were simply inconsistent. Perhaps he lived in the country before and now he's in the city. Or vice versa.

Whatever the case, when you adopt a pet it is *your responsibility* to help him adjust to his new home environment.

My advice on this is to pretend he knows nothing. Teach him everything from scratch, including housebreaking, obedience, manners, etc. Follow the house training methods throughout this book, including personally leash walking, following a food and water schedule, supervising constantly, and confining when necessary.

Another thing to keep in mind is that quite often, rescued dogs are fostered in volunteer's homes before being placed for adoption. These people often work 'round the clock between their regular jobs, rescue volunteering, family obligations, and more...all in the name of doing a good thing. Many obtain the dogs from "death row" at animal shelters and spend significant amounts of their own personal time and money on veterinary care, feeding, training, and other pet care responsibilities.

I think we can all agree that any person who has the heart and dedication to do all that is not likely to be a trickster. They are responsible, caring people who only want to place the dog in an appropriate, permanent home.

If the rescue person told you the dog is housebroken, chances are that it's true! But remember, house training builds off of your pet's instinct not to soil where he *lives*. Since he hasn't lived in your house before, he may not realize at first that this is another living place where he shouldn't go to the bathroom.

Please don't call the rescue people complaining about your dog having an accident. Instead, realize that a re-home adjustment will require some training for every dog, no matter how well house trained he was previously. Be glad that they've done 3/4 of the work for you, and that by simply following a house training schedule, things are likely to be on track in just a few days or weeks.

I thank you, your dog thanks you, and I think I can safely say the rescue people thank you too!

Part III

The Final Stretch

Introduction to
The Final Stretch

     As we approach the end of this book, there are a few more things you may wish to learn about.

     For example, now that your dog is trained, how can you get him to start being more responsible for himself? After all, you don't want to have to be this vigilant forever!

     In this section, we'll address several more concerns that will help you to maximally enjoy your pet for many years to come.

Here we go!

Don't Get a
False Sense of Security

After all the work you've done, you're probably feeling pretty good about your dog by now. Chances are, within just a few days things were getting better already, and within a few weeks, they're looking pretty sharp!

Although I told you to expect your dog to be trained in 30 days or less, you also need to be realistic. Just because the 30th day passed and you flipped the page on the calendar, does not mean you should start letting your dog run free 24/7. You should not stop practicing obedience daily, nor should you discontinue personally walking your dog to the bathroom area.

"What do you mean?", you gasp! What I'm saying is that to end up with a 100% trustworthy dog with free run of the house, you need to reduce your constant supervision *gradually*.

If you want your pet to continue using the designated area on his own without your constant presence, you cannot just suddenly never go out there with him again.

Just as I shared a personal story about my own dog needing some additional training after a move to a new home, so will every pet need sharpening up in some aspect or another throughout his lifetime. No one is perfect, not even your dog.

That said, let's get into more detail about how you should continue from this point forward.

Building to
Free-Run of The House

As this book draws nearer to it's end, you're probably wondering when you can move away from the crate or confinement area, and start giving your dog free run of the house.

This will be largely determined by several factors, including: the age of your dog, his behavior other than house training, and how diligent you've been in following the methods.

For example, if you have a puppy who still goes around nipping furniture, chewing shoes, or doing other mischievous things, you'll likely want to continue with the crate until those issues are completely resolved.

Likewise if you have a puppy or adult dog with separation anxiety or another behavior problem, you may want to continue with confinement until that problem has been brought under control.

However, assuming all other behaviors are fine, and you were only confining for house training purposes, here are some guidelines for building up to free run of the house.

Remember the chapter on Expanding the Den (page 5)? We're building upon the dog's natural instincts not to eliminate where he lives. If you've been following the methods correctly, you've been gradually having your pet to spend time in *every* area of your home (supervised), so he feels like he lives not only in the crate or kitchen, but in the entire house.

After 30 days of diligently following the feeding, watering, walking, and supervision schedule, your dog should definitely not be having any accidents <u>at all</u> in the room of your home where he spends the most time (usually the kitchen). Hopefully he's feeling that way about the entire house, but certainly the kitchen should be his top "keeping clean" priority.

Begin giving freedom gradually. Choose a time when your dog has already eaten, drank water, and did both forms of eliminating outside. Try leaving him in the kitchen with gates up, with his crate door open in case he prefers to go in there. Let him stay loose in there while you clean other parts of your home, take a shower, or do a few household chores.

Assuming all went well on your first try of about 1/2 hour, gradually build up to leaving him loose in the kitchen for up to two hours while you're out. Then try overnight while you're sleeping. If you work, try leaving him loose for the first half of the day, come home at lunch to walk him, and crate him the second half. Then build up to the whole day.

Remember, for the time being, whenever you are home you'll continue to bring him throughout all the other parts of the house on a regular basis, with your supervision.

Once you have your pet to the point where he's got free run of that one area, it's time to expand the den to gradually include another section of your home, and then another. Of course, I've never been to your house, so as I make suggestions please use your own creativity to choose the next most sensible area.

Chances are, your den or living room is another area your pet has spent quite a bit of time in. This would be the next most sensible spot for your dog to have free run after his trustworthiness in the kitchen has been accomplished.

However, you'll need to use your instincts on this one. Does your gut tell you your dog is ready for the living room? Is there wall-to-wall carpeting in there? Will you be able to put a gate up so he's only in the living room and kitchen? Or will free run of the living room equal run of the entire house because there's no way of gating it off? You'll have to use your best judgment in determining the next most logical area to expand the den.

Perhaps your kitchen meets a hallway. Maybe you could move your gate so the dog has free run of the kitchen and the hallway with the doors to the other rooms closed. If things go well, build up to keeping your bathroom, bedroom, or other doors open.

What If My Dog Has An Accident?

If you've been extremely diligent in house training your dog, chances are that he won't have accidents if you expand the den gradually. But it could happen.

Remember, *never ever* correct your dog if you didn't catch him in the act. This could lead to severe house training problems in the future (for a review, see Praise & Correction beginning on page 40, and For Puppies & Older Dogs: Withholding page 77).

Instead, simply clean up the mess, move back to a smaller area for awhile, and put more effort into having him spend supervised time in the "accident room."

To better acclimate your dog and help him feel like the accident room is his home, spend some extra time with him in there over the next few days or weeks. Brush him, practice obedience, play toys with him, snuggle, watch T.V. together, or whatever. The idea is for him to feel like *he lives* in that part of your house too. Maybe even feed him in there so he feels like it's a food area, to be kept clean at all times.

By expanding the den little by little and continuing to personally leash walk, follow a feeding and watering schedule, and supervise when you're home, eventually your dog will have free run. Be patient, and it will pay off in years of enjoying your pet.

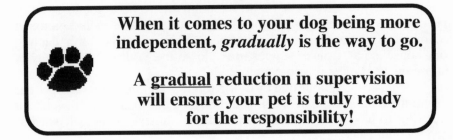

When it comes to your dog being more independent, *gradually* is the way to go.

A <u>gradual</u> reduction in supervision will ensure your pet is truly ready for the responsibility!

Teaching Your Dog to Use the Designated Area on His Own

As I continue through this chapter, please realize that I do not advocate allowing off-leash, neighborhood wandering dogs. As I describe the following methods, please remember that the advice is given with the assumption that either your yard is completely fenced, or you have an underground fence system which your dog has been properly trained to use, or you live on acres and acres of land and your dog never runs off. If none of those apply to you, your pet has no business being off-leash.

You've walked and walked. You've supervised and supervised. You've gone through the extra effort to create a designated bathroom area for your pet in the interest of making it easier to teach him.

Perhaps you'd like to continue enjoying the benefits of a nice, clean yard without having to personally escort your dog every single time for the rest of his life? Understandable!

By now, your dog should be making a beeline straight for his special spot every time he exits the house. At this point, you're basically just along for the company.

You'll need to reduce your supervision *gradually*. Spend the next week or so walking to the area with your dog. Don't put his leash on, but bring it with you anyway. Just seeing it will help your dog remember what to do. Make a conscious effort to use the same body language, and act as if you fully expect your dog to go straight to his area. Praise lavishly as usual.

Assuming things go well, the next week you'll only walk 3/4 of the way to the area, but you'll watch to see that your dog continues on his own. Praise lavishly as usual.

The following week, you'll only walk halfway, and the week after that only 1/4 of the way. Eventually, you'll build up to the point where you're only watching from the door, but your dog continues to the designated area on his own, and you praise lavishly as usual.

At this juncture, you're pretty much home free. You'll need to make sure you keep up with cleaning the designated area very frequently. Remember, if your dog feels like it's dirty, he won't want to go in there. Next thing you know, the area will be getting bigger and bigger until it consumes your whole yard.

Keep things on track by never letting more than one or two poop piles accumulate in there, and sanitizing the area regularly. For a refresher on the recommended upkeep, review Upkeep of the Designated Area (page 21).

Another important part of this process is providing some guidance for your pet on a "free time" basis. This means when you're just hanging around in your yard, playing with your dog or cooking some burgers, you'll need to keep an eye on your pet. Occasionally call him over to the designated area and encourage him to go.

If you see your dog getting ready to urinate or defecate in another part of the yard, *do not correct him*! Doing so could lead to far more serious house training problems than a simple burnt spot on your lawn!

Instead, you can *usher* him over to the designated area, "Max! Come on Max, do your business!" you can call to him as you trot over to the area and encourage him with a whistle or a pat of your thigh.

Hopefully, this will get him trotting right over there with you. If not, no major harm done...he *is* after all, outside. Next time, try to bring him to the area and encourage him to do his business *before* he goes somewhere else on his own. Praise, praise, praise.

Most dogs will fall nicely into using the designated bathroom area on their own by following the methods described in this chapter. Especially if your pet is spayed or neutered, and particularly if you reduce your supervision *gradually*.

If your dog starts to regress at all, simply go back to the leash walking for awhile, or at least personally accompany him to get things back on track.

Teaching Your Dog to Signal When He Needs to Go Out

One of the significantly important things you've been doing throughout the house training process is using the same door each time you and your dog exit the house for a walk to the bathroom area.

Most dogs, after only one or two weeks will begin to at least sit by the door when they need to go out. After 30 days, the majority of dogs will start to signal on their own by either scratching the door or barking. But what if your dog doesn't? You can teach him.

Most breeds or mixes of breeds normally bark to some extent. Unless you have a Basenji (the barkless breed), or a particularly quiet dog, you can teach your dog to "speak" when he needs to go out.

Begin by working with your dog on the "speak" command. Get out a treat that he really loves, like maybe some small pieces of beef jerky. Have your dog "sit," "stay," "down," "give paw," or whatever other commands he knows so you can get him into the learning frame of mind...but don't give him the treats yet.

Next, tell him to "speak." Hold the treat up and tease him a little so he really wants it. As soon as he makes even the tiniest little sound, give the treat and praise "Good boy, speak!" Make the exercise fun. Your pet may start off with just a tiny little whine, and you can build from there to a full-fledged bark.

Once your dog knows the "speak" command, you can transfer that knowledge to the door. Next time you're getting ready to walk your dog, clip his leash on but don't open the door. Get him excited about going out and say "Speak." As soon as he makes even the littlest bark, immediately open the door while petting and praising "Good boy, speak!" You want to make the connection that his bark results in the door opening.

Once your dog has learned the "speak" command, you should not use the treats by the door. The door opening and your praise is reward enough. In fact, if your pet associates the door opening with getting a treat, you could end up with a dog who is constantly barking by the door because he wants a treat. Then you'll have the dilemma of figuring out whether he's only barking because he wants a cookie, or if he really needs to do his business.

Another method that can work, particularly if you have a quiet dog who is not inclined to speak, is to use a bell by the door. Many clients have had excellent results using one of those large parrot cage bells.

Hang it on the door, and whenever your dog wants to go out, lift his paw to tap the bells while saying "Ring." As soon as the bell makes any noise at all, open the door while praising "Good boy, ring!" In time, your dog will begin raising his paw himself and will eventually tap the bells on his own when he needs to go out.

On Your Own

Now that you've read this book in it's entirety, chances are that you have a much better understanding of how dogs think with regard to house training.

I've done my best to provide solutions to many problems...both common and unusual.

Hopefully you will apply the methods, thereby alleviating any house training issues your pet has had, or preventing problems from occurring in the first place.

It's up to you to get the results with your dog. I can write the book. You can buy the book and read it. But if you don't follow the methods, your dog will not become trained.

A funny analogy about dog training is that it's very similar to a gym membership. You can join the gym. You can pay the fee each month, read the brochures, and even wear the t-shirt. You can drive past and say "That's my gym." But if you don't go there and exercise, you're not going to become more fit. Dog training works exactly the same way.

That said, I am confident that you'll take your new found knowledge and put it to good use. You will be vigilant! You will be determined! You will walk and you will supervise!

And soon, you and your pet will have the best possible relationship, enjoying many years of companionship together, without resentment. Enjoy!

About the Author

    Lori Verni is a Certified Master Dog Trainer who has been specializing in family pets since 1995.

    Having received her initial education at the National K-9 School of Dog Trainers, she is qualified to train dogs for obedience, manners, behavior problems, police work, search & rescue, assistance for the handicapped, and much more.

    Noticing that there was a big problem with people not enjoying their pets, enduring years of behavioral issues, and many dogs being relinquished to animal shelters because of behavior, she chose to specialize in family pet training.

    She opened her first dog training school, Best Paw Forward Dog Education, in Long Island, N.Y., in 1995. After two years, her husband Frank Verni, also a Certified Master Trainer, joined her in the business.

    The husband and wife team continued to help pets across Long Island for a total of 10 years before relocating to Holly Springs, N.C. They opened a new Best Paw Forward Dog Education, and have been teaching pets in the Raleigh area since 2004.

    Mrs. Verni has also been a seminar lecturer on dog behavior since 1998. She speaks at colleges, high schools, elementary schools, and youth programs, educating people of all ages about dog behavior.

    Her writing career began in 1997 with the inception of the Best Paw Forward Dog Education Newsletter. Shortly, her writing expanded to include professional assignments which have appeared in numerous magazines, web sites, and newspapers. She is currently a syndicated weekly columnist in four newspapers.

    The dog training couple have been interviewed as experts in their field for various news and television programs, magazines, and pet-related legal cases.

    Well respected by veterinarians, rescue organizations, and pet professionals across the east coast, The Vernis are highly regarded behavior modification professionals who have helped over 3,000 pets and their families.

    The Vernis have two children, one dog, and two cats. This is Mrs. Verni's first book.

Additional Resources

www.FreeDogTrainingInfo.com - This site, owned and operated by the author, contains dozens of free articles on behavioral topics. It's filled with training tips, behavioral guidance, links, and a "pet supplies" section with convenient lists to purchase all of your house training and other pet supply needs. Subscribe to the free newsletter to receive additional training and event information.

www.BestPawOnline.com - For professional dog training services in the Cary, Apex, Holly Springs, Fuquay Varina, Morrisville, and South Raleigh areas of North Carolina only.

www.petsit.com - Pet Sitters International. Search by zip code to find a reputable pet sitter or dog walker near you. Highly recommended for those who work long days and can't get home midday.

www.petfinder.com - Pet Finder is an excellent resource for locating adoptable pets in your area, obtaining shelter and rescue group information, posting a lost or found pet, and much more.

www.akc.org/breeds/rescue.cfm - This address is the breed rescue section of the American Kennel Club's web site, which has a comprehensive listing of rescue groups specifically by breed. Sometimes the contact info listed for the group may not be local to you, but contact them and they'll put you in touch with a local chapter.

To find a reputable dog trainer - Your best resource for finding a reputable trainer is to contact your local veterinarian. Be sure to find out about the trainer's education, experience, and methods.

To purchase additional copies of this book - Visit www.FreeDog TrainingInfo.com and click on "the book" section.

To schedule a book signing, seminar or event - www.FreeDog TrainingInfo.com, and visit the media section or contact us.

Coming Soon

Keep an eye out for Lori Verni's next book, Everything You Need to Know about Dog's Separation Anxiety. Check your local book store, online book store, or subscribe to the free newsletter at www.FreeDogTrainingInfo.com for the announcement of its release!

Made in the USA
Lexington, KY
24 March 2010